A LITTLE
LEARNING
IS A
DANGEROUS
THING

Other quotation books edited by James Charlton

THE WRITER'S QUOTATION BOOK
THE EXECUTIVE'S QUOTATION BOOK
THE MILITARY QUOTATION BOOK
LEGAL BRIEFS

A LITTLE LEARNING IS A DANGEROUS THING

Edited by James Charlton

St. Martin's Press   New York

Library of Congress Cataloging-in-Publication Data

A little learning is a dangerous thing / James Charlton, editor.
          p.   cm.
        ISBN 0-312-11021-9
        1. Education—Quotations, maxims, etc.   I. Charlton, James.
PN6084.E38L57   1994
808.88′2—dc20   94-2043
                                                              CIP

First Edition: June 1994

10 9 8 7 6 5 4 3 2 1

A little learning is a dang'rous thing;
Drink deep, or taste not the Pierian spring:
There shallow draughts intoxicate the brain,
And drinking largely sobers us again.

—ALEXANDER POPE

CONTENTS

INTRODUCTION...xi

AMERICA...1

AS THE TWIG IS BENT...4

CLASSROOMS AND BEYOND...8

COLLEGES AND UNIVERSITIES...14

CURRICULUM...20

EDUCATION...25

EXPERIENCE...31

GENIUS...33

GRADUATION...37

IGNORANCE...42

INTELLECTUALS...44

IVY LEAGUE...47

KNOWLEDGE...50

LEARNING...53

LESSONS...57

METHODOLOGY (OR HOW TO TEACH)...61

MORAL EDUCATION...66

PROFESSORS...70

PUBLIC POLICY...72

READING, 'RITING, 'RITHMETIC...75

REMEMBRANCES...81

SCHOOL...86

STUDENT ATTITUDES...90

CONTENTS

TEACHERS...91
THINKING...98
USES OF EDUCATION...102
VARSITY SPORTS...105
EPITAPHS...109
INDEX...111

I wish to give thanks and A marks to Barbara Binswanger, Maria Robbins, Barbara Anderson, Marian Lizzi, and the people and resources at the Hotchkiss School library.

INTRODUCTION

I went to eleven schools in my youth. Not all in the same town, mind you; my family moved around a lot. The schools ranged from progressive to Roman Catholic, from big city and suburbs to rural, as my parents and I attempted to find the right fit for all of us. I attended one school, in Pennsylvania, for only a day; I spent four years, my longest stint, at New Trier High School. Through all the changes, the many classrooms and teachers good and bad, the one thing that has stayed with me is the intensity of the experience. This rite of passage is particularly vivid because we all meet it with our vulnerabilities and inexperience exposed, our defenses not yet fortified. It is not till later that the scar tissue builds up.

But it is also a time when a gifted and caring instructor can make a difference that can change your life. This is probably the reason that the section of quotations on teachers and teaching is the longest in the book. I could have made an entire volume on this subject, and the request by the book's editor, Barbara Anderson, to trim it was a difficult one to fulfill.

For some, the teenage years were the best years of their life; the period when they were the prettiest, or the most sought after, or the most athletic. For others, that time in grammar and high school is one they wouldn't relive at any price. Many years later, just the sight of a reunion invitation is enough to make them break out in hives and go into a depression for weeks.

College, though, is a great leveler, the best time for most of us. On campus, lifetime friendships are forged, spouses selected, and career directions chosen. It is the time we enter adulthood, or at least have it as an option. Reflecting that, many of the quotes collected here have to do with the collegiate life of scholars, students, and professors.

I have long since graduated, though I am involved in schools as a parent and occasional teacher. *A Little Learning* is meant to be amusing and entertaining to both students and teachers. But I suggest it also has a message, albeit a small one: that continued learning for ourselves is vital, and that the teaching of others is one of the most important jobs in any civilized society. For me, my education goes on daily. As Eartha Kitt wisely said, "The tombstone will be my diploma."

JAMES CHARLTON
New York City

America is the best half-educated country in the world.

—NICHOLAS MURRAY BUTLER

AMERICA

Americans have always had an ambivalent attitude toward intelligence. When they feel threatened, they want a lot of it, and when they don't they regard the whole thing as somewhat immoral.

—VERNON A. WALTERS

There is no underestimating the intelligence of the American public.

—H. L. MENCKEN

It is ironic that the United States should have been founded by intellectuals for throughout most of our political history the intellectual has been for the most part either an outsider, a servant, or a scapegoat.

—RICHARD HOFSTADTER

Why do most Americans look up to education and look down upon educated people?

—SYDNEY J. HARRIS

Americans are the only people in the world known to me whose status anxiety prompts them to advertise their college and university affiliations in the rear window of their automobiles.

—PAUL FUSSELL

The idea of a college education for all young people of capacity, provided at a nominal cost by their own states, is very peculiarly American. We in America invented the idea. We in America have developed it with remarkable speed.

—LYNDON B. JOHNSON

It is our American habit if we find the foundations of our educational structure unsatisfactory to add another story or wing. We find it easier to add a new study or course or kind of school than to re-organize existing conditions so as to meet the need.

—JOHN DEWEY

America has always chosen to secure an adequate number of teachers not with money or status, but by making it easy to become a teacher. America has never really tried to make teaching an attractive lifetime occupation.

—DAN LORTI

The business of the American teacher is to liberate American citizens to think apart and act together.

—STEPHEN S. WISE

What are our schools for if not an indoctrination against Communism?

—RICHARD NIXON

Those who worry about radicalism in our schools and colleges are often either reactionaries who themselves do not bear allegiance to the traditional American principles, or defeatists who despair of the success of our own philosophy in an open competition.

—JAMES BRYANT CONANT

We are quite rich enough to defend ourselves, whatever the cost. We must now learn that we are quite rich enough to educate ourselves as we need to be educated.

—WALTER LIPPMANN

Ignorant people in preppy clothes are more dangerous to America than oil embargoes.

—V. S. NAIPAUL, after a year of college teaching

Our progress as a nation can be no swifter than our progress in education. . . . The human mind is our fundamental resource.

—JOHN F. KENNEDY

No one worries about kids going out for football and competing to be on the team—that's ability grouping, and so is the band and cheerleading squad. But when we do these things in academics, it becomes "undemocratic, un-American."

—CAROL MILLS, Johns Hopkins University Center for talented youth

This will never be a civilized country until we expend more money for books than we do for chewing gum.

—ELBERT HUBBARD

As the
Twig is
Bent . . .

'Tis education forms the common mind:
Just as the twig is bent, the tree's inclined.

—ALEXANDER POPE

A scholar is of all persons the most unfit to teach young children. A mother is the infant's true guide to knowledge.

—EDWARD BULWER-LYTTON

A good education is the next best thing to a pushy mother.

—CHARLES SCHULZ, "Peanuts"

A child educated only at school is an uneducated child.

—GEORGE SANTAYANA

Education begins at home. You can't blame school for not putting into your child what you don't put into him.

—GEOFFREY HOLDER

Bringing up children and training horses aren't so terribly different. With horses it's no good letting them boss you around in the stable and expect them to be saints outside. Same with children. It's no good letting them come home from school and rampage around the house and then express surprise that their school report says they're too boisterous. On the whole, animals are easier, because they don't answer back.

—PRINCESS ANNE

4

I mean a child that doesn't have a parent to read to that child or that doesn't see that when the child is hurting to have a parent and help out or neither parent there enough to pick the kid up and dust him off and send him back into the game or whatever, that kid has a disadvantage.

—GEORGE BUSH

If there were no schools to take the children away from home part of the time, the insane asylums would be filled with mothers.

—EDGAR W. HOWE

In a child's lunch box, a mother's thought.

—Japanese proverb

The only people who seem to have nothing to do with the education of the children are the parents.

—G. K. CHESTERTON

Parents have become so convinced that educators know what is best for children that they forget that they themselves are really the experts.

—MARIAN WRIGHT EDELMAN

Helping your eldest to pick a college is one of the greatest educational experiences of life—for the parents. Next to trying to pick his bride, it's the best way to learn that your authority, if not entirely gone, is slipping fast.

—SALLY RESTON and JAMES RESTON

Your responsibility as a parent is not as great as you might imagine. You need not supply the world with the next conqueror of disease or major motion picture star. If your child simply grows up to be someone who does not use the word "collectible" as a noun, you can consider yourself an unqualified success.

—FRAN LEIBOWITZ

Our schools are still set up as though every mother were at home all day and the whole family needed the summer to get the crops in.

—SIDNEY CALLAHAN

The only reason I always try to meet and know the parents better is because it helps me to forgive their children.

—LOUIS JOHANNOT

If you promise not to believe everything your child says happens at this school, I'll promise not to believe everything he says happens at home.

—ANONYMOUS

Children are remarkable for their intelligence and ardor, for their curiosity, their intolerance of shams, the clarity and ruthlessness of their vision.

—ALDOUS HUXLEY

How is it that little children are so intelligent and men so stupid? It must be education that does it.

—ALEXANDRE DUMAS

Education is helping a child realize his potentialities.

—ERICH FROMM

I am beginning to suspect all elaborate and special systems of education. They seem to me to be built upon the supposition that every child is a kind of idiot who must be taught to think. Whereas, if the child is left to himself, he will think more and better.

—ANNE SULLIVAN

No one has yet fully realized the wealth of sympathy, kindness and generosity hidden in the soul of a child. The effort of every true education should be to unlock that treasure.

—EMMA GOLDMAN

Children who are treated as if they are uneducable almost invariably become uneducable.

—KENNETH B. CLARK

What we want is to see the child in pursuit of knowledge, and not knowledge in pursuit of the child.

—GEORGE BERNARD SHAW

Children, like animals, use all their senses to discover the world.

—EUDORA WELTY

CLASSROOMS AND BEYOND

All I ever really need to know I learned in kindergarten.

—ROBERT FULGHUM

I see the mind of the 5-year-old as a volcano with two vents: destructiveness and creativeness.

—SYLVIA ASHTON-WARNER

The real menace in dealing with a five-year-old is that in no time at all you begin to sound like a five-year-old.

—JEAN KERR

[School is] a kind of state-supported baby-sitting service.

—GERALD KENNEDY

Grammar school never taught me anything about grammar.

—ISAAC GOLDBERG

I only went to the third grade because my father only went to fourth and I didn't want to pass him.

—DIZZY DEAN

I quit school in the fifth grade because of pneumonia. Not because I had it but because I couldn't spell it.

—ROCKY GRAZIANO

Still, if nobody dropped out at the eighth grade, who would be ready to hire the college graduates?

—*Chatham* (ONTARIO) *News*

The hen
has a nest.
The hen has the
best nest.
The hen can
rest on the nest.

There is nothing on earth intended for innocent people so horrible as a school. It is in some respects more cruel than a prison. In prison, for example, you are not forced to read books written by the warders and the governor.

— GEORGE BERNARD SHAW

Thou hast most traitorously corrupted the youth of the realm in erecting a grammar school.

— WILLIAM SHAKESPEARE, *The Second Part of Henry the Sixth*

It used to take me all vacation to grow a new hide in place of the one they flogged off me during school term.

— MARK TWAIN

There is less flogging in our great schools than formerly, but then less is learned there; so that what boys get at one end they lose at the other.

— SAMUEL JOHNSON

All the learnin' my father ever paid for was a bit o' birch at one end and an alphabet at the other.

— GEORGE ELIOT

In my day, Mother packed a banana in your lunchbox, and you had to use that as a pistol to fake it when attempting a heist or a mugging. Today, it seems, the box contains Teflon-coated .38-caliber specials along with the trail gorp.

— NICHOLAS VON HOFFMAN

A suburban junior high school cafeteria is like a microcosm of the world. The goal is to protect yourself, and safety comes in groups. You had your cool kids, you had your smart kids, you had your greasers. In effect, in junior high school, who you are is defined less by who you are than who is the person next to you.

—FRED SAVAGE, *The Wonder Years*

True terror is to wake up one morning and discover that your high school class is running the country.

—KURT VONNEGUT

A realistic high school counselor teaches kids to get ready for disappointment.

—CAROL BLY

I have often wondered about two things. First, why high school kids almost invariably hate the books they are assigned to read by their English teachers, and second, why English teachers almost invariably hate the books students read in their spare time. Something seems very wrong with such a situation. There is a bridge out here, and the ferry service is uncertain at best.

—STEPHEN KING

There's nothing wrong with teenagers, that reasoning with them won't aggravate.

—ANONYMOUS

When I was seventeen or so,
I scoffed at money grubbers.
I had cold contempt for dough,
and I wouldn't wear my rubbers.

— OGDEN NASH

Think before you speak. Read before you think. This will give you something to think about that you didn't make up yourself—a wise move at any age, but most especially at seventeen, when you are in the greatest danger of coming to annoying conclusions.

— FRAN LEIBOWITZ

As I vaguely recall from my own experience, adolescence was a time when you firmly believed that sex hadn't been invented until the year you started high school, when the very idea that anything interesting might have happened during your parents' lifetime was unthinkable.

— RUSSELL BAKER

The poet, as everyone knows, must strike his individual note sometime between the ages of fifteen and twenty-five. He may hold it a long time, or a short time, but it is then that he must strike it or never. School and college have been conducted with the almost express purpose of keeping him busy with something else till the danger of his ever creating anything is past.

— ROBERT FROST

At sixteen I was stupid, confused and indecisive. At twenty-five I was wise, self-confident, prepossessing and assertive. At forty-five I am stupid, confused, insecure and indecisive. Who would have supposed that maturity is only a short break in adolescence?

—JULES FEIFFER

In my early years I read very hard. It is a sad reflection, but a true one, that I knew almost as much at eighteen as I do now.

—SAMUEL JOHNSON

Between eighteen and twenty, life is like an exchange where one buys stocks, not with money, but with actions. Most men buy nothing.

—ANDRÉ MALRAUX

I knew at fifteen pretty much what I wanted to do . . . I resolved that at thirty I would know more about poetry than any man living.

—EZRA POUND

When I was a boy of fourteen, my father was so ignorant I could hardly stand to have the old man around. But when I got to be twenty-one, I was astonished at how much the old man had learned in seven years.

—MARK TWAIN

Develop your eccentricities while you are young. That way, when you are old, people won't think you're going ga-ga.

—DAVID OGILVY

COLLEGES AND UNIVERSITIES

The scramble to get into college is going to be so terrible in the next few years that students are going to put up with almost anything, even an education.

—BARNABY KEENEY, president, Brown University

I am not impressed by the Ivy League establishments. Of course they graduate the best—it's all they'll take, leaving to others the problem of educating the country. They will give you an education the way the banks will give you money—provided you can prove to their satisfaction that you don't need it.

—PETER DE VRIES

In your temporary failure there is no evidence that you may not yet be a better scholar, and a great more successful man in the struggle of life, than many others, who have entered college more easily.

—ABRAHAM LINCOLN, in a letter to George C. Lathan after the young man's application to Harvard was rejected.

The quality of a university is measured more by the kind of student it turns out than the kind it takes in.

—ROBERT J. KIBBEE

Any college that would take your son he should be too proud to go to.

—ERMA BOMBECK

A university education cannot be handed out complete like a cake on a tray. It has to be fought for, intrigued for, conspired for, lied for, and sometimes simply stolen. If it has not, it would scarcely be education.

—ARNOLD BENNETT

It is not enough to offer a smorgasbord of courses. We must insure that the students are not eating just at one end of the table.

—A. BARTLETT GIAMATTI

A society that thinks the choice between ways of living is just a choice between equally eligible "lifestyles" turns universities into academic cafeterias offering junk food for the mind.

—GEORGE WILL

They teach you anything in universities these days. You can major in mudpies.

—ORSON WELLES

When a subject becomes totally obsolete we make it a required course.

—PETER DRUCKER

The function of the university is not simply to teach bread-winning, or to furnish teachers for the public schools or to be a center of polite society; it is, above all, to be the organ of that fine adjustment between real life and the growing knowledge of life, an adjustment which forms the secret of civilization.

—W. E. B. DUBOIS

A university should be a place of light, of liberty, and of learning.

—BENJAMIN DISRAELI

A university studies politics, but it will not advocate fascism or communism. A university studies military tactics, but it will not promote war. A university studies peace, but it will not organize crusades of pacifism.

—LOTUS DELTA COFFMAN

The college was not founded to give society what it wants. Quite the contrary.

—MAY SARTON

The university is simply the canary in the coal mine. It is the most sensitive barometer of social change.

—JAMES PERKINS

Freedom of inquiry, freedom of discussion, and freedom of teaching—without these a university cannot exist.

—ROBERT MAYNARD HUTCHINS

Universities are full of knowledge; the freshmen bring a little in and the seniors take away none at all, and the knowledge accumulates.

—ABBOTT LAWRENCE LOWELL

A university is an institution of higher yawning.
—LEONARD L. LEVINSON

A place where pebbles are polished and diamonds are dimmed.
—ROBERT G. INGERSOLL

A university is a college with a stadium seating over 40,000.
—LEONARD L. LEVINSON

A university is what a college becomes when the faculty loses interest in the students.
—JOHN CIARDI

If a man is a fool, you don't train him out of being a fool by sending him to university. You merely turn him into a trained fool, ten times more dangerous.
—DESMOND BAGLEY

If you have both feet planted on level ground, then the university has failed you.
—ROBERT F. GOHEEN

No man should escape our universities without knowing how little he knows.
—J. ROBERT OPPENHEIMER

There was no place I could go to cut classes.
—MARVIN BARNES, on why he earned so many college credits in prison

It takes most men five years to recover from a college education, and to learn that poetry is as vital to thinking as knowledge.

—BROOKS ATKINSON

At college age you can tell who is best at taking tests and going to school, but you can't tell who the best people are. That worries the hell out of me.

—BARNABY KEENEY, president, Brown University

Colleges are like old age homes, except for the fact that more people die in colleges.

—BOB DYLAN

Fathers send their sons to college either because they went to college or they didn't.

—L. L. HENDREN

[The shortage of student loans] may require . . . divestiture of certain sorts—stereo divestiture, automobile divestiture, three-weeks-at-the-beach divestiture.

—WILLIAM J. BENNETT

Economists report that a college education adds many thousands of dollars to a man's lifetime income—which he then spends sending his son to college.

—BILL VAUGHAN

College is the best time of your life. When else are your parents going to spend several thousand dollars a year just for you to go to a strange town and get drunk every night?

—DAVID WOOD

Teenagers go to college to be with their boyfriends and girlfriends; they go because they can't think of anything else to do; they go because their parents want them to and sometimes because their parents don't want them to; they go to find themselves, or to find a husband, or to get away from home, and sometimes even to find out about the world in which they live.

—HAROLD HOWE

I find that the three major administrative problems on a campus are sex for the students, athletics for the alumni, and parking for the faculty.

—CLARK KERR

College for women was a refinement whose main purpose was to better prepare you for your ultimate destiny . . . to make you a more desirable product.

—PAT LOUD

The dream of college apparently serves as a substitute for more direct preoccupation with marriage: girls who do not plan to go to college are more explicit in their desire to marry, and have a more developed sense of their own sex role.

—ELIZABETH DOUVAN

Never get married in college; it's hard to get a start if a prospective employer finds you've already made one mistake.

—ELBERT HUBBARD

In American society, the university is traditionally considered to be a psychosocial moratorium, an ivory tower where you withdraw from the problems of society and the world around you to work on important things like your career and marriage.

—ABBIE HOFFMAN

College is a place to keep warm between high school and an early marriage.

—GEORGE GOBEL

CURRICULUM

A classic is something that everybody wants to have read and nobody wants to read.

—MARK TWAIN

The classics are only primitive literature. They belong in the same class as primitive machinery and primitive medicine.

—STEPHEN LEACOCK

Every man with a belly full of the classics is an enemy of the human race.

—HENRY MILLER

So they told me how Mr. Gladstone read Homer for fun, which I thought served him right.

—WINSTON CHURCHILL

Nobody can say a word against Greek; it stamps a man at once as an educated gentleman.

—GEORGE BERNARD SHAW

A gentleman need not know Latin, but he should at least have forgotten it.

—BRANDER MATTHEWS

If the Romans had been obliged to learn Latin, they would never have found time to conquer the world.

—HEINRICH HEINE

One attraction of Latin is that you can immerse yourself in the poems of Horace and Catullus without fretting over how to say, "Have a nice day."

—PETER BRODIE

Tim was so learned that he could name a horse in nine languages: so ignorant that he bought a cow to ride on.

—BENJAMIN FRANKLIN

Modern man is educated to understand foreign languages and misunderstand foreigners.

—G. K. CHESTERTON

America is the only country left where we teach languages so that no pupil can speak them.

—ALFRED KAZIN

Impoverished writers remind me of Somerset Maugham's remark about multilingual people. He admired them, he said, but did not find that their condition made them necessarily wise.

— GRAHAM GREENE

In college, they major in Business Administration. If, to meet certain requirements, they have to take a liberal arts course, they take Business Poetry.

— DAVE BARRY, on Yuppies

History teaches us that men and nations behave wisely once they have exhausted all other alternatives.

— ABBA EBAN

History does not repeat itself. Historians repeat each other.

— ARTHUR BALFOUR

That men do not learn from history is the most important of all lessons that history has to teach.

— ALDOUS HUXLEY

To remain ignorant of what happened before you were born is to remain always a child.

— MARCUS TULLIUS CICERO

Over! It's not over till we say it's over! Was it over when the Germans bombed Pearl Harbor?

— JOHN BELUSHI, in the movie *Animal House*

I was terrible at history. I could never see the point of learning what people thought way back when.

For instance, the ancient Phoenicians believed that the sun was carried across the sky on the back of an enormous snake. So what? So they were idiots.

—DAVE BARRY

History is philosophy teaching by example.

—DIONYSIUS

The object of philosophy is the logical clarification of thought.

—LUDVIG WITTGENSTEIN

If you've never met a student from the University of Chicago, I'll describe him to you. If you give him a glass of water, he says, "This is a glass of water. But is it a glass of water? And if it is a glass of water, why is it a glass of water?" And eventually he dies of thirst.

—SHELLEY BERMAN

I was thrown out of college for cheating on the metaphysics exam: I looked into the soul of another boy.

—WOODY ALLEN

If I had to live my life over again, I would elect to be a trader of goods rather than a student of science. I think barter is a noble thing.

—ALBERT EINSTEIN

Science is always wrong. It never solves a problem without creating ten more.

—GEORGE BERNARD SHAW

Science robs men of wisdom and usually converts them into phantom beings loaded up with facts.

— MIGUEL DE UNAMUNO Y JUGO

The simplest schoolboy is now familiar with truths for which Archimedes would have sacrificed his life.

— ERNEST RENAN

The term Science should not be given to anything but the aggregate of the recipes that are always successful. All the rest is literature.

— PAUL VALÉRY

Schools are loath to teach the role of sex in classics like *Romeo and Juliet*. They ought to level. His (Shakespeare's) themes are timeless.

— MORGAN FREEMAN

The best kind of sex education is life in a loving family.

— ROSEMARY HAUGHTON

The best sex education for kids is when Daddy pats Mommy on the fanny when he comes home from work.

— DR. WILLIAM H. MASTERS

Sex in the hands of public educators is not a pretty thing.

— KEVIN ARNOLD

Education is learning what you didn't know you didn't know.

—GEORGE BOAS

EDUCATION

An education isn't how much you've committed to memory, or even how much you know. It's being able to differentiate between what you know and what you don't. It's knowing where to go to find out what you need to know; and it's knowing how to use the information you get.

—WILLIAM FEATHER, attributed

Education bewildered me with knowledge and facts in which I was only mildly interested.

—CHARLIE CHAPLIN

Education is an admirable thing, but it is well to remember from time to time that nothing that is worth knowing can be taught.

—OSCAR WILDE

Education is an ornament in prosperity and a refuge in adversity.

—ARISTOTLE

Education is simply the soul of a society as it passes from one generation to another.

—G. K. CHESTERTON

Education is the ability to listen to almost anything without losing your temper or your self-confidence.

—ROBERT FROST

Education is the process of casting false pearls before real swine.

—IRWIN EDMAN

Education is what happens to the other person, not what comes out of the mouth of the educator.

—MILES HORTON

Education is what survives when what has been learned has been forgotten.

—B. F. SKINNER

Education, *n.* That which discloses to the wise and disguises from the foolish their lack of understanding.

—AMBROSE BIERCE, *The Devil's Dictionary*

Education, then beyond all other devices of human origin, is the great equalizer of the conditions of men—the balance-wheel of the social machinery.

—HORACE MANN

Education . . . has produced a vast population able to read but unable to distinguish what is worth reading.

—G. M. TREVELYAN

Education: the inculcation of the incomprehensible into the indifferent by the incompetent.

—JOHN MAYNARD KEYNES

He is educated who knows how to find out what he doesn't know.

—GEORGE SIMMEL, German philosopher

Human history becomes more and more a race between education and catastrophe.

—H. G. WELLS

I consider a human soul without an education like
marble in a quarry, which shows none of its inher-
ent beauties until the skill of the polisher sketches
out the colors, makes the surface shine, and discovers every ornamental cloud, spot, and vein that runs
through it.

—JOSEPH ADDISON

I read Shakespeare and the Bible, and I can shoot
dice. That's what I call a liberal education.

—TALLULAH BANKHEAD

I wonder whether if I had had an education I should
have been more or less a fool than I am.

—ALICE JAMES

I had no patience with schooling and formal education. I dropped out of college in my freshman
year and became a full-time disc jockey.

—RUSH LIMBAUGH

If I had learned education I would not have had
time to learn anything else.

—CORNELIUS VANDERBILT

It is always an advantage not to have received a
sound commercial education.

—OSCAR WILDE

No man who worships education has got the best out of education. . . . Without a gentle contempt for education no man's education is complete.

—G. K. CHESTERTON

Real education must ultimately be limited to men who INSIST on knowing, the rest is mere sheep-herding.

—EZRA POUND

Sixty years ago I knew everything; now I know nothing; education is a progressive discovery of our own ignorance.

—WILL DURANT

The chief wonder of education is that it does not ruin everybody concerned in it, teachers and taught.

—HENRY BROOKS ADAMS

The gains of education are never really lost; Books may be burned and cities sacked, but truth, like the yearning for freedom, lives in the hearts of humble men.

—FRANKLIN ROOSEVELT

They realized that education was not a thing of one's own to do with what one pleases—that it was not a personal privilege to be merely enjoyed by the possessor—but a precious treasure transmitted; a sacred trust to be held, used, and enjoyed, and if possible, strengthened—then passed on to others upon the same trust.

—LOUIS BRANDEIS

29

To be able to be caught up in the world of thought—that is being educated.

—EDITH HAMILTON

We need education in the obvious more than investigation of the obscure.

—OLIVER WENDELL HOLMES, JR.

You know that education is one thing that can't be taken away from you. Nobody can rob you of your education, because it is in your head; that is, if you have any head and are capable of holding it. Most of us are capable of holding an education, if we try to get it.

—HARRY TRUMAN

I derive my education from the uneducated.

—GEORGE BERNARD SHAW

I prefer the company of peasants because they have not been educated sufficiently to reason incorrectly.

—MICHEL EYQUEM DE MONTAIGNE

None of us got where we are solely by pulling ourselves up by our bootstraps. We got here because somebody—a parent, a teacher, an Ivy League crony or a few nuns—bent down and helped us pick up our boots.

—THURGOOD MARSHALL

The things taught in school are not an education but the means to an education.

—RALPH WALDO EMERSON

Do you know the difference between education and experience? Education is when you read the fine print; experience is what you get when you don't.

—PETE SEEGER

Like most self-taught men, he overestimated the value of an education.

—RICHARD HENRY DANA

I have never let my schooling interfere with my education.

—MARK TWAIN

Any place that anyone young can learn something useful from someone with experience is an educational institution.

—AL CAPP

The great difficulty in education is to get experience out of ideas.

—GEORGE SANTAYANA

A man who carries a cat by the tail learns something he can learn in no other way.

—MARK TWAIN

You can get help from teachers, but you are going to have to learn a lot by yourself, sitting alone in a room.

—THEODORE GEISEL (DR. SEUSS)

I was thinking that we all learn by experience but some of us have to go to summer school.

— PETER DE VRIES

I think everyone should go to college and get a degree and then spend six months as a bartender and six months as a cabdriver. Then they would really be educated.

— AL MCGUIRE

An MBA's first shock could be the realization that companies require experience before they hire a chief executive officer.

— ROBERT HALF

A whale ship was my Yale College and my Harvard.

— HERMAN MELVILLE

[Experience is] a good school, but the fees are high.

— HEINRICH HEINE

Suffering is overrated. It doesn't teach you anything.

— BILL VEECK

Experience is the name everyone gives to their mistakes.

— OSCAR WILDE

The hardest thing to learn in life is which bridge to cross and which to burn.

— DAVID L. RUSSELL

Experience is the worst teacher; it gives the test before presenting the lesson.

—VERNON LAW

Everyone is a genius at least once a year. The real geniuses simply have their bright ideas closer together.

—GEORG CHRISTOPH LICHTENBERG

GENIUS

Intelligence recognizes what has happened. Genius recognizes what will happen.

—JOHN CIARDI

Genius, in truth, means little more than the faculty of perceiving in an unhabitual way.

—WILLIAM JAMES

There are one-story intellects, two-story intellects, and three-story intellects with skylights. All fact collectors with no aim beyond their facts are one-story men. Two-story men compare, reason, and generalize, using labors of the fact collectors as well as their own. Three-story men idealize, imagine, and predict. Their best illuminations come from above through the skylight.

—OLIVER WENDELL HOLMES, SR.

When a true genius appears in the world, you may know him by this sign, that the dunces are all in confederacy against him.

—JONATHAN SWIFT

33

Genius is more often found in a cracked pot than in a whole one.

—E. B. WHITE

It takes a lot of time to be a genius, you have to sit around so much doing nothing, really doing nothing.

—GERTRUDE STEIN

Every child is born a genius.

—R. BUCKMINSTER FULLER

One is not born a genius. One becomes a genius.

—SYLVIA ASHTON-WARNER

A genius? Perhaps, but before I was a genius, I was a drudge.

—IGNACE JAN PADEREWSKI

Genius is one percent inspiration and ninety-nine percent perspiration.

—THOMAS ALVA EDISON

If there is such a thing as genius, which is just what—what the fuck is it?—I am one, you know. And if there isn't, I don't care.

—JOHN LENNON

You study, you learn, but you guard the original naiveté. It has to be within you, as desire for drink is within the drunkard or love is within the lover.

—HENRI MATISSE

A harmless hilarity and a buoyant cheerfulness are not infrequent concomitants of genius; and we are never more deceived than when we mistake gravity for greatness, solemnity for science, and pomposity for erudition.

—CHARLES CALEB COLTON

Creative minds always have been known to survive any kind of bad training.

—ANNA FREUD

What does education often do? It makes a straight-cut ditch out of a free, meandering brook.

—HENRY DAVID THOREAU

Originality is the essence of true scholarship. Creativity is the soul of the true scholar.

—NNAMDI AZIKIWE

The invention of IQ does a great disservice to creativity in education.

—JOEL HILDEBRAND

It's a scientific fact that if you stay in California you lose one point of your IQ every year.

—TRUMAN CAPOTE

The high IQ has become the American equivalent of the Legion of Honor, positive proof of the child's intellectual aristocracy. . . . It has become more important to be a smart kid than a good kid or even a healthy kid.

—SAM LEVENSON

At eight or nine, I suppose, intelligence is no more than a small spot of light on the floor of a large and murky room.

—H. L. MENCKEN

What a distressing contrast there is between the radiant intelligence of the child and the feeble mentality of the average adult.

—SIGMUND FREUD

I've always felt that a person's intelligence is directly reflected by the number of conflicting points of view he can entertain simultaneously on the same topic.

—LISA ALTHER

The test of a first-rate intelligence is the ability to hold two opposed ideas in the mind at the same time, and still retain the ability to function. One should, for example, be able to see that things are hopeless and yet be determined to make them otherwise.

—F. SCOTT FITZGERALD

Intelligence appears to be the thing that enables a man to get along without education. Education enables a man to get along without the use of his intelligence.

—ALBERT EDWARD WIGGAM

It has yet to be proved that intelligence has any survival value.

—ARTHUR C. CLARKE

We pay a high price for being intelligent. Wisdom hurts.

—EURIPIDES

We should take care not to make the intellect our god; it has, of course, powerful muscles, but no personality.

—ALBERT EINSTEIN

Just about a month from now I'm set adrift, with a diploma for a sail and lots of nerve for oars.

—RICHARD HALLIBURTON

GRADUATION

Finals, the very name of which implies that nothing of importance can happen after it.

—DAVID LODGE

Graduation is like being born—traumatic, but inevitable. It means you have to decide upon a profession that you can talk about at future social gatherings.

—LISA BIRNBACH

Indeed one of the ultimate advantages of education is simply coming to an end of it.

—B. F. SKINNER

I never graduated from Iowa. I was only there for two terms—Truman's and Eisenhower's.

—ALEX KARRAS

37

I tell every kid I talk to that they should make sure they get a college education before signing a pro contract. You don't have to know anything to get a college degree, but if you've got one, people think you're intelligent.

—CAL GRIFFITH, Minnesota Twins owner

No, but they gave me one anyway.

—ELDEN CAMPBELL, pro basketball player, when asked if he earned a degree from Clemson University

This job is better than I could get if I used my college degree, which, at this point, I can't remember what it was in.

—BOB GOLIC, football player, on signing a pro contract for $1.5 million

Don't get a college degree. You don't need it in the theatre. It is a waste of four years.

—ORSON BEAN

I decided to become an actor because I was failing in school and I needed the credits.

—DUSTIN HOFFMAN

Those who learn for grades expect to succeed in their business. Today they are right in so far as almost every American who has a degree, however ignorant, can live better than even competent people in much poorer countries. . . . But this cannot last long in the situation when "competence" and a diploma tautologically mean each other. . . . Some-

day ignorant people with degrees and diplomas may want power according to their papers rather than real competence.

—ANDREI TOOM

Some men are graduated from college *cum laude*, some are graduated *summa cum laude*, and some are graduated *mirabile dictu*.

—WILLIAM HOWARD TAFT

I had not the advantage of a classical education, and no man should, in my judgment, accept a degree he cannot read.

—MILLARD FILLMORE, upon declining a degree from Oxford University

It's an insane tragedy that 700,000 people get a diploma each year and can't read the damned diploma.

—WILLIAM BROCK

Nothing is as easy to make as a promise this winter to do something next summer: this is how commencement speakers are caught.

—SYDNEY J. HARRIS

The commencement speaker is like a corpse at a funeral. You can't have a commencement without one, and no one expects you to say much.

—ROBERT DOLE

Commencement oratory must eschew anything that smacks of partisan politics, political preference, sex, religion, or unduly firm opinion. Nonetheless, there must be a speech: Speeches in our culture are the vacuum that fills the vacuum.

—JOHN KENNETH GALBRAITH

If you just went with someone who is popular with students, you'd have Madonna and all sorts of degenerates. When I invited Elie Weisel, I doubt many students even knew who he was.

—JOHN SILBER, president, Boston University, on why he doesn't consult students on the choice of commencement speakers

The Greeks had their laurel wreaths. The English have their honors lists. The French are always wearing ribbons in their lapels. In this country honorary degrees from universities serve that function.

—JACK PELTASON

It might be said now that I have the best of both worlds. A Harvard education and a Yale degree.

—JOHN F. KENNEDY, on receiving an honorary degree from Yale, June 12, 1963

I'm going right home to tell my parents. They always wanted a doctor in the family.

—GEORGE BURNS, age ninety-seven, upon receiving an honorary degree from Brandeis University

IGNORANCE

A muttonhead, after an education at West Point—or Harvard—is a muttonhead still.

—THEODORE ROOSEVELT

Poverty has many roots, but the tap root is ignorance.

—LYNDON B. JOHNSON

Everybody is ignorant, only on different subjects.

—WILL ROGERS

Ignorance is a right! Education is eroding one of the few democratic freedoms remaining to us.

—CHRISTOPHER ANDREA

Ignorance is not bliss—it is oblivion.

—PHILIP WYLIE

Ignorance is of a peculiar nature; once dispelled, it is impossible to re-establish it. It is not originally a thing in itself, but is only the absence of knowledge; and though man may be kept ignorant, he cannot be made ignorant.

—THOMAS PAINE

Our knowledge can only be finite, while our ignorance must necessarily be infinite.

—KARL POPPER

The ignorant classes are the dangerous classes. Ignorance is the womb of monsters.

—HENRY WARD BEECHER

I know some people think I'm stupid, but my parents didn't raise no dummies. Hey, there are dif-

42

ferent kinds of intelligence. Albert Einstein was bad in English. Of course, Einstein was German.

—BOB KEARNEY

I live by Louis Pasteur's advice that "Chance favors the prepared mind," and my own, "The two most common elements in the known universe are hydrogen and stupidity."

—HARLAN ELLISON

There is nothing so stupid as the educated man if you get him off the thing he was educated in.

—WILL ROGERS

The trouble with the world is that the stupid are cocksure and the intelligent are full of doubt.

—BERTRAND RUSSELL

It's not the most intellectual job in the world, but I do have to know the letters.

—VANNA WHITE

It is possible for a student to win twelve letters at a university without his learning how to write one.

—ROBERT MAYNARD HUTCHINS

If you think education is expensive, try ignorance.

—DEREK BOK

INTELLECTUALS

He's very clever, but sometimes his brains go to his head.

— MARGOT ASQUITH

They say that we are better educated than our parents' generation. What they mean is that we go to school longer. They are not the same thing.

— RICHARD YATES

Very few people can stand the strain of being educated without getting superior over it.

— STEPHEN LEACOCK

An educated man ... is thoroughly inoculated against humbug, thinks for himself, and tries to give his thoughts, in speech or on paper, some style.

— ALAN SIMPSON

Erudition, *n.* Dust shaken out of a book into an empty skull.

— AMBROSE BIERCE, *The Devil's Dictionary*

That is the worst of erudition—that the next scholar sucks the few drops of honey that you have accumulated, sets right your blunders, and you are superseded.

— A. C. BENSON

It is not for nothing that the scholar invented the Ph.D. thesis as his principal contribution to the literary form. The Ph.D. thesis is the perfect image of his world. It is work done for the sake of doing work—perfectly conscientious, perfectly laborious, perfectly irresponsible.

— ARCHIBALD MACLEISH

The average Ph.D. thesis is nothing but a transference of bones from one graveyard to another.

—J. FRANK DOBIE

A learned man is an idler who kills time by study.

—GEORGE BERNARD SHAW

I too had thoughts once of being an intellectual, but I found it too difficult.

—ALBERT SCHWEITZER

The world's great men have not commonly been great scholars, nor great scholars great men.

—OLIVER WENDELL HOLMES, SR.

It is a woeful mistake to suppose that the educated are kinder and more tolerant: education creates vested interests, and renders the beneficiaries jealous and very vocal.

—LEWIS BERNSTEIN NAMIER

[An intellectual] is someone who can listen to the "William Tell Overture" without thinking of the Lone Ranger.

—JOHN CHESSON

[An intellectual is] a man who takes more words than necessary to tell us more than he knows.

—DWIGHT D. EISENHOWER

A decade after graduation, almost everyone will have forgotten when and where and what they played. But every time they speak, everyone will know whether they are educated.

—REVEREND THEODORE HESBURGH, president, Notre Dame

College ain't so much where you been as how you talk when you get back.

—OSSIE DAVIS, *Purlie Victorious*

"Whom are you?" said he, for he had been to night school.

—GEORGE ADE

As far as I'm concerned, "whom," is a word that was invented to make everyone sound like a butler.

—CALVIN TRILLIN

Lack of education is an extraordinary handicap when one is being offensive.

—JOSEPHINE TEY

When ideas fail, words come in very handy.

—JOHANN WOLFGANG VON GOETHE

I've overeducated myself in all the things I shouldn't have known.

—NOEL COWARD

Once you're educated above a certain point, to the rest of the world you're a big sissy.

—PAUL RUDNICK

A highbrow is a person educated beyond his intelligence.

—BRANDER MATTHEWS

She was the most over-read girl I have ever known, but she still said "Between you and I."

— ROBERTSON DAVIES

Only in show business could a guy with a C-minus average be considered an intellectual.

— MORT SAHL, talking about himself

To liberals, to beat somebody on the field is morally aggressive. . . . If we ever won the Ivy League title, the administration would have us investigated by the American Civil Liberties Union.

— D. KEITH MANO, on Columbia football

IVY LEAGUE

Columbia was in the game right up to the national anthem.

— JIM NANCE, on Columbia's thirty-fifth straight loss

If I ask a kid how he did on the boards, and he says 12 a game, I know he's not coming to Harvard.

— PETER ROBY, Harvard basketball coach

Gentlemen, you are about to play Harvard. Never in your life will you do anything so important.

— T. A. D. JONES, Yale football coach

Four years was enough of Harvard. I still had a lot to learn, but had been given the liberating notion that now I could teach myself.

— JOHN UPDIKE

47

Harvard is primarily a place where you tear apart the theories others have made.

—JERRY HARRISON, Talking Heads guitarist and keyboard player

If I had done everything I'm credited with, I'd be speaking to you from a laboratory jar at Harvard.

—FRANK SINATRA

I understand that Harvard University is making its diplomas either larger or smaller. I have forgotten which. This is a step in the right direction.

—ROBERT MAYNARD HUTCHINS

Studying literature at Harvard is like learning about women at the Mayo Clinic.

—ROY BLOUNT, JR.

I would rather be governed by the first 300 names in the Boston telephone book than by the faculty of Harvard University.

—WILLIAM F. BUCKLEY, JR.

I spoke at the long-haired college of Harvard; I told them we got people in Alabama as intelligent and refined and cultured as you are and don't you ever forget it. I made the best speech they ever heard up at Harvard and, you know, the next day hundreds of them got their hair cut.

—GEORGE WALLACE

To be a Princeton man is an enviable distinction.

—JOHN F. KENNEDY, on his Princeton admissions application, 1935

Do you know what my own story is? Well, I was always the poorest boy at a rich man's school. Yes, it was that way at prep schools, and at Princeton, too.

—F. SCOTT FITZGERALD

Princeton is a wonderful little spot; a quaint ceremonious village of puny demigods on stilts.

—ALBERT EINSTEIN

My favorite University is Princeton ... and yet, I believe that were all education above the high school level suspended for ten years, humanity would get a better chance to be what humanitarian Princeton itself could wish to be.

—FRANK LLOYD WRIGHT

KNOWLEDGE

I will have no intellectual training. Knowledge is ruin among my young men.

—ADOLF HITLER

A man should keep his little brain attic stocked with all the furniture that he is likely to use and the rest he can put away in the lumber-room of his library, where he can get at it if he wants it.

—ARTHUR CONAN DOYLE

I was at that age when a man knows least and is most vain of his knowledge; and when he is ex-

50

tremely tenacious in defending his opinion upon subjects about which he knows nothing.

—WASHINGTON IRVING

It is better to know some of the questions than to know all the answers.

—JAMES THURBER

Knowledge is knowing as little as possible.

—CHARLES BUKOWSKI

Like sex, knowledge is good if used in the service of life and love.

—LILLIAN SMITH

Much knowledge does not teach wisdom.

—HERACLITUS

The trouble with people is not that they don't know but that they know so much that ain't so.

—JOSH BILLINGS

We are here and now. Further than that, all knowledge is moonshine.

—H. L. MENCKEN

If money is your hope for independence, you will never have it. The only real security a man can have in this world is a reserve of knowledge, experience, and ability.

—HENRY FORD

"Know thyself?" If I knew myself, I'd run away.

—JOHANN WOLFGANG VON GOETHE

I am the only person in the world I should like to know thoroughly.

—OSCAR WILDE

Know thyself! A maxim as pernicious as it is ugly. Whoever observes himself arrests his own development. A caterpillar who wanted to know itself well would never become a butterfly.

—ANDRÉ GIDE

I am astounded by people who want to "know" the universe when it's hard enough to find your way around Chinatown.

—WOODY ALLEN

Good people are good because they've come to wisdom through failure. We get very little wisdom from success, you know.

—WILLIAM SAROYAN

The art of being wise is the art of knowing what to overlook.

—WILLIAM JAMES

Wisdom is not wisdom when it derives from books alone.

—HORACE

Education is a private matter between the person and the world of knowledge and experience, and has little to do with school or college.

—LILLIAN SMITH

A little learning is a dang'rous thing;
Drink deep, or taste not the Pierian spring:
There shallow draughts intoxicate the brain,
And drinking largely sobers us again.

—ALEXANDER POPE

If a little knowledge is dangerous, where is the man
who has so much as to be out of danger?

—T. H. HUXLEY

A Little Learning *misleadeth*, and a great deal often
stupifieth the Understanding.

—GEORGE SAVILE

A little learning, indeed, may be a dangerous thing,
but the want of learning is a calamity to any people.

—FREDERICK DOUGLASS

His had been an intellectual decision founded on
his conviction that if a little knowledge was a dangerous thing, a lot was lethal.

—TOM SHARPE

Abandon learning, and you will be free from trouble and distress.

—LAO-TSE

Learning is its own exceeding great reward.

—WILLIAM HAZLITT

You have learned something. That always feels at
first as if you had lost something.

—H. G. WELLS

That is what learning is. You suddenly understand something you've understood all your life, but in a new way.

— DORIS LESSING

The important thing is not so much that every child should be taught, as that every child should be given the wish to learn.

— JOHN LUBBOCK

In the traditional method the child must say something that he has merely learned. There is all the difference in the world between having something to say, and having to say something.

— JOHN DEWEY

If you wish to be agreeable in society, you must consent to be taught many things which you know already.

— CHARLES MAURICE DE TALLEYRAND

I am always ready to learn although I do not always like being taught.

— WINSTON CHURCHILL

"I dunno," Arthur said. "I forget what I was taught. I only remember what I've learnt."

— PATRICK WHITE

They know enough who know how to learn.

— HENRY BROOKS ADAMS

Man can learn nothing except by going from the known to the unknown.

—CLAUDE BERNARD

Never learn anything until you find that you have been uncomfortable for a long while by not knowing it.

—SAMUEL BUTLER

Never learn to do anything: if you don't learn, you always find someone else to do it for you.

—MARK TWAIN

No one is ever old enough to know better.

—HOLBROOK JACKSON

Students, whatever their age, rarely are young.

—EDWARD BULWER-LYTTON

The man who is too old to learn was probably always too old to learn.

—HENRY S. HASKINS

All that I know I learned after I was thirty.

—GEORGES CLEMENCEAU

It's what you learn after you know it all that counts.

—JOHN WOODEN

The brighter you are the more you have to learn.

—DON HEROLD

Don't tell me because they're poor, don't tell me that because they live in a certain section, don't tell me because they come from single parents, don't tell me because they're immigrant that they cannot learn.

—RAMON CORTINES, chancellor, New York City Schools

A boy can learn a lot from a dog: obedience, loyalty, and the importance of turning around three times before lying down.

—ROBERT BENCHLEY

Learning, *n.* The kind of ignorance distinguishing the studious.

—AMBROSE BIERCE, *The Devil's Dictionary*

Learning is the art of knowing how to use common sense to advantage.

—JOSH BILLINGS

There are understandings that expand, not imperceptibly hour by hour, but as certain flowers do, by little explosive ruptures, with periods of quiescence in between.

—GEORGE WASHINGTON CABLE

We're drowning in information and starving for knowledge.

—RUTHERFORD D. ROGERS

You can't learn too soon that the most useful thing about a principle is that it can always be sacrificed to expediency.

—SOMERSET MAUGHAM

Wear your learning like your watch, in a private pocket; and do not pull it out, and strike it, merely to show that you have one.

—LORD CHESTERFIELD

The only way I can make five A's is when I sign my name.

—ALAA ABDELNABY, commenting on his academic career while at Duke University

The players on the Maryland football team all made straight As. Their Bs were a little crooked.

—JOHNNY WALKER

I think the world is run by C students.

—AL MCGUIRE

My suggestion that we have a constitutional amendment making a C average a requirement for the presidency brought me mail from [Dan Quayle's] supporters. The letters are quite stirring. They say things like, "He's probably not as dumb as all that."

—CALVIN TRILLIN

You know, I'm not so sure that we want all those that graduated number one or number two in their class to be on . . . our federal judiciary. This is a diversified society.

—DAN QUAYLE

You can get all A's and still flunk life.

—WALKER PERCY

There is a story of an applicant for admission to a famous graduate school, who, when asked by the Dean of Admissions whether he had graduated in the upper half of his college class—replied with great pride: "Sir, I belong to that section of the class which makes the upper half of the class possible."

—JULIUS COHEN

Doctors and lawyers must go to school for years and years, often with little sleep and with great sacrifice to their first wives.

—ROY BLOUNT, JR.

If law school is so hard to get through, how come there are so many lawyers?

—CALVIN TRILLIN

I had the worst study habits and the lowest grades. Then I found out what I was doing wrong. I had been highlighting with a black Magic Marker.

—JEFF ALTMAN

The best thing about baseball is that there's no homework.

—DAN QUISENBERRY

"That's the reason they're called lessons," the Gryphon remarked, "because they lesson from day to day."

—LEWIS CARROLL, *Alice in Wonderland*

PICTORIAL ALPHABET.

A a	AX ax	E e	ELK elk
B b	BOX box	F f	FAN fan
C c	CAT cat	G g	GIRL girl
D d	DOG dog	H h	HEN hen

The way to do research is to attack the fact at the point of greatest astonishment.

—CELIA GREEN

Copy from one it's plagiarism; copy from two, it's research.

—WILSON MIZNER

I find people call it research nowadays if they ever have to look up anything in a book.

—MARGARET LANE

What is research, but a blind date with knowledge.

—WILL HENRY

He who devotes sixteen hours a day to hard study may become at sixty as wise as he thought himself at twenty.

—MARY WILSON LITTLE

It doesn't make much difference what you study, as long as you don't like it.

—PETER FINLEY DUNNE

Just as eating against one's will is injurious to health, so study without a liking for it spoils the memory, and it retains nothing it takes in.

—LEONARDO DA VINCI

Examinations, sir, are pure humbug from beginning to end. If a man is a gentleman he knows quite enough, and if he is not a gentleman whatever he knows is bad for him.

—OSCAR WILDE

I have this terrible fear that I'm going to be forced to take a general knowledge test in public.

— DICK CAVETT

I had great verbal SATs, but I was so bad at math I assumed any college would say, "Well, we just won't ask him to add."

— PAUL RUDNICK

You must realize that honorary degrees are given generally to people whose SAT scores were too low to get them into schools the regular way. As a matter of fact, it was my SAT scores that led me into my present vocation in life, comedy.

— NEIL SIMON

Like is to *like* as *like* is to ____?

— CALVIN TRILLIN, on the best SAT analogy question for his daughter

---

The mediocre teacher tells. The good teacher explains. The superior teacher demonstrates. The great teacher inspires.

— WILLIAM ARTHUR WARD

Good teaching is one-fourth preparation and three-fourths theater.

— GAIL GODWIN

METHODOLOGY
(OR HOW TO
TEACH)

A good teacher, like a good entertainer first must hold his audience's attention. Then he can teach his lesson.

—HENDRIK JOHN CLARKE

The main fact about education is that there is no such thing. Education is a word like "transmission" or "inheritance"; it is not an object, but a method.

—G. K. CHESTERTON

The perfect method of learning is analogous to infection. It enters and spreads.

—LEO STEIN

The forcing of Latin, geometry, and algebra in a certain kind of manner into a certain kind of head is not education; it is persecution.

—FRANK MOORE COLBY

To me education is a leading out of what is already there in the pupil's soul. To Miss Mackay it is a putting in of something that is not there, and that is not what I call education. I call it intrusion.

—MURIEL SPARK, *The Prime of Miss Jean Brodie*

In teaching it is the method and not the content that is the message . . . the drawing out, not the pumping in.

—ASHLEY MONTAGUE

Education is not filling a pail but the lighting of a fire.

—WILLIAM BUTLER YEATS

Feed a man a fish and you've fed him for a day. Teach a man to fish and you've fed him for a lifetime.

—Saying

Give a man a fish, and he can eat for a day. But teach a man how to fish, and he'll be dead of mercury poisoning inside of three years.

—CHARLES HAAS

Much education today is monumentally ineffective. All too often we are giving young people cut flowers when we should be teaching them to grow their own plants.

—JOHN W. GARDNER

Spoon feeding in the long run teaches us nothing but the shape of the spoon.

—E. M. FORSTER

Why is it today that we seem to be afraid of urging kids on to excellence and achievement? Our society is more inclined to let kids develop at their own pace—not push them too hard.

—RUSH LIMBAUGH

The chief object of education is not to learn things but to unlearn things.

—G. K. CHESTERTON

What is really important in education is not that the child learns this and that, but that the mind is matured, that energy is aroused.

—SØREN KIERKEGAARD

Too often we give children answers to remember rather than problems to solve.

—ROGER LEWIN

We have learned the answers, all the answers: It is the question that we do not know.

—ARCHIBALD MACLEISH

Questions are never indiscreet. Answers sometimes are.

—OSCAR WILDE

Law students can learn more from knowing how to ask good questions than from studying appellate briefs.

—ANTHONY AMSTERDAM

The study of laws, on condition they are good laws, is unrivaled in its ability to improve the student.

—PLATO

Women are educated—who knows how?—as it were by breathing in ideas, by living rather than by acquiring knowledge. The status of manhood, on the other hand, is attained only by the stress of thought and much technical exertion.

—G. W. FRIEDRICH HEGEL

I hear and I forget.
I see and I remember.
I do and I understand.

—Chinese proverb

Training is everything. The peach was once a bitter almond; cauliflower is nothing but cabbage with a college education.

—MARK TWAIN

Teaching is the only major occupation of man for which we have not yet developed tools that make an average person capable of competence and performance. In teaching we rely on the "naturals," the ones who somehow know how to teach.

—PETER DRUCKER

The most extraordinary thing about a really good teacher is that he or she transcends accepted educational methods. Such methods are designed to help average teachers approximate the performance of good teachers.

—MARGARET MEAD

The teacher should never lose his temper in the presence of the class. If a man, he may take refuge in profane soliloquies; if a woman, she may follow the example of one sweet-faced and apparently tranquil girl—go out in the yard and gnaw a post.

—WILLIAM LYON PHELPS

The object of teaching a child is to enable him to get along without his teacher.

—ELBERT HUBBARD

Give me a girl at an impressionable age, and she is mine for life.

—MURIEL SPARK, *The Prime of Miss Jean Brodie*

The true teacher defends his pupils against his own personal influence.

—A. B. ALCOTT

A teacher who is not dogmatic is simply a teacher who is not teaching.

—G. K. CHESTERTON

It is nothing short of a miracle that the modern methods of instruction have not entirely strangled the holy curiosity of enquiry.

—ALBERT EINSTEIN

Some people excuse bad teaching by saying: Since students buy it, it is OK to sell it. But pushers of drugs say the same. It is the responsibility of specialists to do the right things even if laymen cannot discriminate between right and wrong.

—ANDREI TOOM

We have ignored cultural literacy in thinking about education. . . . We ignore the air we breathe until it is thin or foul. Cultural literacy is the oxygen of social intercourse.

—E. D. HIRSCH, JR.

MORAL
EDUCATION

Teaching kids to count is fine, but teaching them what counts is best.

—BOB TALBERT

Education does not mean teaching people to know what they do not know; it means teaching them to behave as they do not behave.

—JOHN RUSKIN

66

Prejudices, it is well known, are most difficult to eradicate from the heart whose soil has never been loosened or fertilized by education; they grow there, firm as weeds among stones.

—CHARLOTTE BRONTË

An educated man is one who has the right loves and hatreds.

—LIN YUTANG

The first idea that the child must acquire, in order to be actively disciplined, is that of the difference between good and evil; and the task of the educator lies in seeing that the child does not confound good with immobility and evil with activity.

—MARIA MONTESSORI

Education is not the means of showing people how to get what they want. Education is an experience by means of which enough men, it is hoped, will learn to want what is worth having.

—RONALD REAGAN

Education is a method by which one acquires a higher degree of prejudice.

—LAWRENCE J. PETER

The highest result of education is tolerance.

—HELEN KELLER

Real education should educate us out of self into something far finer—into selflessness which links us with all humanity.

—NANCY ASTOR

Respect for the fragility and importance of an individual life is still the first mark of the educated man.

—NORMAN COUSINS

The child learns more of the virtues needed in modern life—of fairness, of justice, of comradeship, of collective interest and action—in a common school than can be taught in the most perfect family circle.

—CHARLOTTE PERKINS GILMAN

If any man will sum us up according to our actions and behavior, he will find many more excellent men among the educated; I mean as regards to virtue.

—MICHEL EYQUEM DE MONTAIGNE

The want of education and moral training is the only real barrier that exists between classes of men.

—SUSANNA MOODIE

The first quality of a good education is good manners—and some people flunk the course.

—HUBERT HUMPHREY

The only good advice is a good example. You don't tell them a whole lot of anything. You show them by doing. You teach values by making choices in their presence. They see what you do and they make judgments on it.

—OSSIE DAVIS

There is no moral problem here—I used to teach ethics. Trust me.

—WILLIAM J. BENNETT, on the notion of decapitation for drug dealers.

I would advise no one to send his child where the Holy Scriptures are not supreme. . . . I greatly fear that the Universities, unless they teach the Holy Scriptures diligently and impress them on the young students, are wide gates to hell.

—MARTIN LUTHER

The parents have a right to say that no teacher paid by their money shall rob their children of faith in God, and send them back to their homes skeptical, or infidels, or agnostics, or atheists.

—WILLIAM JENNINGS BRYAN

PROFESSORS

A professor is one who talks in someone else's sleep.

—W. H. AUDEN

Professors simply can't discuss a thing. Habit compels them to give a lecture.

—HAL BOYLE

Most educators would continue to lecture on navigation while the ship is going down.

—JAMES H. BOREN

If one cannot state a matter clearly enough so that even an intelligent twelve-year-old can understand it, one should remain within the cloistered walls of the university and laboratory until one has a better grasp of one's subject.

—MARGARET MEAD

Some experience of popular lecturing had convinced me that the necessity of making things plain to uninstructed people was one of the very best means of clearing up the obscure corners in one's own mind.

—T. H. HUXLEY

My method of teaching precluded any genuine contact with my students. At best they regurgitated a few bits of my brain during examination.

—VLADIMIR NABOKOV

Professors must have a theory as a dog must have fleas.

—H. L. MENCKEN

The dons are too busy educating the young men to be able to teach them anything.

—SAMUEL BUTLER

Academic education is the act of memorizing things read in books, and things told by college professors who got their education mostly by memorizing things read in books.

—ELBERT HUBBARD

Culture is an instrument wielded by professors to manufacture professors, who when their turn comes, will manufacture professors.

— SIMONE WEIL

Tenure has alleviated one major source of insecurity—and has removed one major tool of quality control; in many places it is virtually impossible to fire a teacher who hasn't committed a criminal offense.

— TRACY KIDDER

University politics are vicious because the stakes are so small.

— HENRY KISSINGER

PUBLIC
POLICY
———

We call our schools free because we are not free to stay away from them until we are sixteen years of age.

— ROBERT FROST

I look for a day when education will be like the landscape, free for all. Beauty and truth should be free to everyone who has the capacity to absorb. The private school, the private library, the private art gallery, the exclusive college, have got to go. We want no excellence that is not for all.

— ELBERT HUBBARD

A democratic form of government, a democratic way of life, presupposes free public education over a long period; it presupposes also an education for personal responsibility that too often is neglected.

—ELEANOR ROOSEVELT

Poverty must not be a bar to learning and learning must offer an escape from poverty.

—LYNDON B. JOHNSON

There is one sin that slavery committed against me which I can never forgive. It robbed me of my education. The injury is irreparable.

—JAMES W. C. PENNINGTON

Education remains the key to both economic and political empowerment. That is why the schools which are in charge of educating African Americans have, perhaps, the longest, the greatest, the deepest challenges of all . . . to get into the minds of young African Americans so that they who recognize opportunity will come to those who are prepared.

—BARBARA JORDAN

Education is indoctrination if you're white—subjugation if you're black.

—JAMES BALDWIN

Education is the cheap defense of nations.

—EDMUND BURKE

By educating the young generation along the right lines, the People's State will have to see to it that a generation of mankind is formed which will be adequate to this supreme combat that will decide the destinies of the world.

—ADOLF HITLER

Why should we subsidize intellectual curiosity?

—RONALD REAGAN

I question whether we can afford to teach mother macramé when Johnny still can't read.

—JERRY BROWN

Modern cynics and skeptics . . . see no harm in paying those to whom they entrust the minds of their children a smaller wage than is paid to those to whom they entrust the care of their plumbing.

—JOHN F. KENNEDY

If Chrysler had an assembly line in which the same number of cars got through as kids do in our school system, people would be scandalized.

—FRANK MACCHIAROLA, chancellor, New York City Schools

We are not asking our children to do their own best but to be the best. Education is in danger of becoming a religion based on fear; its doctrine is to compete. The majority of our children are being led to believe that they are doomed to failure in a world which has room only for those at the top.

—EDA J. LESHAN

Jefferson thought schools would produce free men: we prove him right by putting dropouts in jail.

—BENJAMIN R. BARBER

When I was a boy on the Mississippi River there was a proposition in a township to discontinue public schools because they were too expensive. An old farmer spoke up and said if they stopped the schools they would not save anything, because every time a school was closed a jail had to be built.

—MARK TWAIN

The man who reads nothing at all is better educated than the man who reads nothing but newspapers.

—THOMAS JEFFERSON

The regular course was Reeling and Writhing, of course, to begin with; and then the different branches of Arithmetic—Ambition, Distraction, Uglification, and Derision.

—LEWIS CARROLL

Reading furnishes the mind only with the materials of knowledge; it is thinking makes what we read ours.

—JOHN LOCKE

Oh! what blockheads are those wise persons who think it necessary that a child should comprehend everything he reads.

—ROBERT SOUTHEY

READING,
'RITING,
'RITHMETIC

I took a speed reading course and read *War and Peace* in twenty minutes. It's about Russia.

—WOODY ALLEN

Education is what you learn in books, and nobody knows you know it but your teacher.

—VIRGINIA CARY HUDSON

I told the Englishman that my alma mater was books, a good library. Every time I catch a plane, I have with me a book that I want to read. And that's a lot of books. If I weren't out there every day battling the white man, I could spend the rest of my life reading. Just to satisfy my curiosity.

—MALCOLM X

Books were my pass to personal freedom. I learned to read at age three, and soon discovered there was a whole world to conquer that went beyond our farm in Mississippi.

—OPRAH WINFREY

I must say I find television very educational. The minute somebody turns it on, I go to the library and read a good book.

—GROUCHO MARX

Educational television should be absolutely forbidden. It can only lead to unreasonable expectations and eventual disappointment when your child discovers that the letters of the alphabet do not leap up

76

out of books and dance around the room with royal-blue chickens.

—FRAN LEIBOWITZ

The young, with their keen noses for hypocrisy, are in fact adept readers—but not of books. They are society-smart rather than school smart. Their teachers in that world, the nation's true pedagogues, are television, advertising, movies, politics, and the celebrity domains they define.

—BENJAMIN R. BARBER

There is only one thing that can kill the Movies and that is education.

—WILL ROGERS

I never went to college. But I have lectured on campuses for a quarter-century, and it is my impression that after taking a course in The Novel, it is an unusual student who would ever want to read a novel again.

—GORE VIDAL

Our American professors like their literature clear and cold and pure and very dead.

—SINCLAIR LEWIS

Everywhere I go I'm asked if I think the university stifles writers. My opinion is that they don't stifle enough of them. There's many a bestseller that could have been prevented by a good teacher.

—FLANNERY O'CONNOR

I did not begin to write novels until I had forgotten all I had learned at school and college.

—JOHN GALSWORTHY

Teaching has ruined more American novelists than drink.

—GORE VIDAL

Poetry is so vital to us until school spoils it.

—RUSSELL BAKER

Most people on this continent can read and write in some degree, though the number of those who cannot is disgracefully large. An astonishing number of those who can read and write think that they do so rather well.

—ROBERTSON DAVIES

I tell you, I find fan mail really depressing. I mean the grammatical errors, the spelling errors I see, and I'm not being a stickler about this.

—BEBE NEUWIRTH

All the people I have in my office, they can't speak English properly. All the letters sent from my office I have to correct myself, and that is because English is taught so bloody badly.

—PRINCE CHARLES

Fluency in English is something that I'm not often accused of.

—GEORGE BUSH

One has to be able to count, if only so that at fifty, one doesn't marry a girl of twenty.

—MAXIM GORKY

The only way I can distinguish
proper from improper fractions
Is by their actions.

—OGDEN NASH

As far as the laws of mathematics refer to reality, they are not certain, and as far as they are certain, they do not refer to reality.

—ALBERT EINSTEIN

I never did very well in math—I could never seem to persuade the teacher that I hadn't meant my answers literally.

—CALVIN TRILLIN

I like mathematics because it is not human and has nothing particular to do with this planet or with the whole accidental universe—because, like Spinoza's God, it won't love us in return.

—BERTRAND RUSSELL

Numbers constitute the only universal language.

—NATHANIEL WEST

Stand firm in your refusal to remain conscious during algebra. In real life, I assure you, there is no such thing as algebra.

—FRAN LEIBOWITZ

What is algebra exactly; is it those three-cornered things?

—J. M. BARRIE

It is hard to convince a high-school student that he will encounter a lot of problems more difficult than those of algebra and geometry.

—EDGAR W. HOWE

When we reach the sphere of mathematics we are among processes which seem to some the most in-human of all human activities and the most remote from poetry. Yet it is there that the artist has fullest scope for his imagination.

—HAVELOCK ELLIS

REMEMBRANCES

This school was on top of a hill so that God could see everything that went on. It looked like a cross between a prison and a church and it was.

—QUENTIN CRISP

My early years in school were quite miserable. I had a stammer and I wrote with my left hand. So I was made to sit in the back of the room and could move up only as my stammer improved and I switched to my right hand.

—MAURICE SENDAK

The year I started school, when I was four, I had difficulty making the numeral two. Every time I made it backwards, my teacher hit me on the knuckles. The more she did this, the more I could never get it right. I can see her standing over me in her blue dress with alphabets and numbers on it. I don't remember anything any other teacher wore.

— MARVA COLLINS

I am going back because it was a very good school and I was happy there, and because I hope I can give back a little to the students who have taken my place, perhaps teach them that not all writers are old English guys, mostly dead.

— ANNA QUINDLEN

I took a little English, a little math, some science, some hubcaps, and some wheel covers.

— GATES BROWN, Detroit Tiger outfielder, recalling high school

I started attending Emory College in Atlanta—I majored at Emory in Beer, with a minor in Rock 'n Roll.

— MAC DAVIS

I had a reputation as a "brain" in high school. I was the girl who never combed her hair—I never even got asked to my senior prom. I remember my junior year I got a *B* in algebra, and I was devastated for weeks. I didn't understand the courage it takes to admit your mistakes. Now I know to admit what I don't know. That's the first step toward learning more.

— DIANE SAWYER

Ever since I was a little girl I wanted to go to college, and I didn't think there was a reason to forgo my dream of an academic life to pursue a film career. I would rather have my education and know who Dostoevski is than have a beach house in Malibu.

—JENNIFER BEALS

People like me are aware of their so-called genius at ten, eight, nine. I always wondered, "why has nobody discovered me?" In school, didn't they see that I'm cleverer than anybody in this school? That the teachers are stupid, too? That all they had was information that I didn't need.

—JOHN LENNON

I did my first characterization in Bernards High School. Not in a school play, but in school. I did a complete, conscious transformation of myself. I dyed my hair, got contacts, and became the perfect magazine-page knockout. For several years I played the part of the blond homecoming queen. It was a wonderful time, but I wish I hadn't taken things so seriously.

—MERYL STREEP

We were never allowed to cross our legs. This was something I don't understand, particularly as I got older and it seemed to me that that should be exactly what they would want us to do. But the nuns insisted that crossed legs were legs that commanded attention and apparently legs are something that induce men to sin.

— GINA CASCONE

When I was in high school, I earned the pimple award and every other gross-out award. My friends always enjoyed me, and I retaliated with my tongue. I was nicknamed The Weaver, meaning one who weaves magical sentences. In my last year of school, I was voted Class Optimist and Class Pessimist. Looking back, I realize I was only half right.

— JACK NICHOLSON

In ninth grade my dream was to beat my brother Larry at a game of one-on-one. He'd beat me every time and I'd get mad. In tenth grade my dream was to make the varsity team, but I didn't and I had to play junior varsity all year. When I look back on these experiences, I know they must have built determination in me.

— MICHAEL JORDAN

Not making the baseball team at West Point was one of the greatest disappointments of my life, maybe the greatest.

— DWIGHT D. EISENHOWER

I have often thought that if there had been a good rap group around in those days, I might have chosen a career in music rather than politics.

— RICHARD NIXON

Ambition: To join Little Richard.

—BOB DYLAN's high school yearbook, class of '59

In hindsight, I probably didn't enjoy my major. I didn't want to teach; I wanted to entertain. I wanted an audience that wanted to be there instead of had to be there.

—GENE SIMMONS, of Kiss

I never studied fashion design. I think cheerleading affected my career the most.

—BETSEY JOHNSON

My whole freshman year I wore brown and white shoes. Actually, they were impractical, because the white one kept getting dirty.

—DICK CAVETT

My blissful childhood ended abruptly when I was sent at 12 to one of the most severe and traditional private schools in New England. I was the first or second Jewish student ever to go there. I used to think, "Why did they admit me?" and figured it must be because I was a good student. The worst thing happened at year's end, when I was ranked first in my class and in the school. I thought from then on, "Well, that's what I have to do." I couldn't relax. It was really misery.

—JONATHAN KOZOL

I learned three important things in college—to use a library, to memorize quickly and visually, to drop asleep at any time given a horizontal surface and fifteen minutes. What I could not learn was to think creatively on schedule.

—AGNES DEMILLE

Convents do the same thing progressive schools do, only they don't know it. They don't teach you to read; you have to find out for yourself. . . . But as for helping me in the outside world, the convent taught me only that if you spit on a pencil eraser, it will erase ink.

—DOROTHY PARKER

SCHOOL

But, good gracious, you've got to educate him first. You can't expect a boy to be vicious till he's been to a good school.

—SAKI (H. H. MUNRO)

The founding fathers in their wisdom decided that children were an unnatural strain on parents. So they provided jails called schools, equipped with tortures called education. School is where you go when your parents can't take you and industry can't take you.

—JOHN UPDIKE

You send your child to the schoolmaster, but 'tis the schoolboys who educate him.

—RALPH WALDO EMERSON

86

I always loved learning and hated school.

—I. F. STONE

The schools ain't what they used to be and never was.

—WILL ROGERS

Great schools are little societies.

—HENRY FIELDING

A school should not be a preparation for life. A school should be life.

—ELBERT HUBBARD

Public schools are the nurseries of all vice and immorality.

—HENRY FIELDING

Of all the cursed places under the sun, where the hungriest soul can hardly pick up a few grains of knowledge, a girl's boarding school is the worst. They are called finishing schools, and the name tells accurately what they are. They finish everything but imbecility and weakness, and that they cultivate.

—OLIVE SCHREINER

All our schools are finishing schools; they finish what has never been begun.

—G. K. CHESTERTON

87

And yet, in the schoolroom more than any other place, does the difference of sex, if there is any, need to be forgotten.

—SUSAN B. ANTHONY

Show me a man who has enjoyed his school days and I will show you a bully and a bore.

—ROBERT MORLEY

School days, I believe, are the unhappiest in the whole span of human existence. They are full of dull, unintelligible tasks, new and unpleasant ordinances, brutal violations of common sense and common decency.

—H. L. MENCKEN

I was a modest, good-humored boy; it is Oxford that has made me insufferable.

—MAX BEERBOHM

If a boy be of a mischievous, wicked inclination, no school will ever make him good.

—HENRY FIELDING

I can say that anyone who, like me, has been educated in English public schools and served in the ranks of the British army is quite at home in a Third World prison.

—ROGER COOPER, upon his release after five years in an Iranian prison

His English education at one of the great public schools had preserved his intellect perfectly and permanently at the stage of boyhood.

—G. K. CHESTERTON

British education is probably the best in the world if you can survive it. If you can't there's nothing left for you, but the diplomatic corps.

—PETER USTINOV

We class schools you see, into four grades: Leading School, First-rate School, Good School, and School.

—EVELYN WAUGH

In actual fact, Prep schools are as eager to indoctrinate their students with the Preppy Morality as they are to get them into the right colleges. Catalogs speak of teaching students self-discipline, responsibility, and a quality called intellectual rigor. These schools are forming good citizens as well as good students—or so they'd like to think.

—LISA BIRNBACH

Work 'em hard, play 'em hard, feed 'em up to the nines, and send 'em to bed so tired that they are asleep before their heads are on the pillow.

—FRANK L. BOYDEN, headmaster, Deerfield Academy

STUDENT
ATTITUDES

We are students of words: we are shut up in schools, and colleges, and recitation-rooms, for ten or fifteen years, and come out at last with a bag of wind, a memory of words, and do not know a thing.

—RALPH WALDO EMERSON

I never dared be radical when young
For fear it would make me conservative
when old.

—ROBERT FROST

The most conservative persons I ever met are college undergraduates.

—WOODROW WILSON

A young man who is not a radical about something is a pretty poor risk for education.

—JACQUES BARZUN

When I was a student at the Sorbonne in Paris I used to go out and riot occasionally. I can't remember now which side it was on.

—JOHN FOSTER DULLES

If our colleges and universities do not breed men who riot, who rebel, who attack life with all the youthful vim and vigor, then there is something wrong with our colleges. The more riots that come on college campuses, the better world for tomorrow.

—WILLIAM ALLEN WHITE

The most dangerous thing about student riots is that adults take them seriously.

—GEORGES POMPIDOU

Campus agitators are rarely, if ever, students or faculty from the scientific disciplines; they tend to come out of the social sciences, which are relatively inexact in their researches, and the humanities, which are and should be preoccupied with unanswerable questions.

—SAMUEL B. GOULD

Anyone who refuses to speak out off campus does not deserve to be listened to on campus.

—REVEREND THEODORE HESBURGH, president, Notre Dame

It is important that students bring a certain ragamuffin, barefoot irreverence to their studies; they are not here to worship what is known, but to question it.

—JACOB BRONOWSKI

How anybody dresses is indicative of his self-concept. If students are dirty and ragged, it indicates that they are not interested in tidying up their intellects either.

—S. I. HAYAKAWA

He is either dead or teaching school.

—ZENOBIUS

Everybody who is incapable of learning has taken to teaching—that is really what our enthusiasm for education has come to.

—OSCAR WILDE

TEACHERS

He who can, does. He who cannot, teaches.

—GEORGE BERNARD SHAW

If you can't do, teach. If you can't teach, teach phys-ed.

—ANONYMOUS

You don't have to think too hard when you talk to a teacher.

—J. D. SALINGER

The vanity of teaching often tempts a man to forget he is a blockhead.

—LORD HALIFAX

Teaching is not a lost art, but the regard for it is a lost tradition.

—JACQUES BARZUN

He that teaches himself hath a fool for a master.

—BENJAMIN FRANKLIN

The schoolteacher is certainly underpaid as a child minder, but ludicrously overpaid as a teacher.

—JOHN OSBORNE

In teaching you cannot see the fruit of a day's work. It is invisible and remains so, maybe for twenty years.

—JACQUES BARZUN

One good teacher in a lifetime may sometimes change a delinquent into a solid citizen.

—PHILIP WYLIE

I touch the future. I teach.

—CHRISTA MCAULIFFE

A teacher affects eternity; he can never tell where his influence stops.

—HENRY BROOKS ADAMS

A teacher should have maximal authority, and minimal power.

—THOMAS SZAZ

Don't try to fix the students, fix ourselves first. The good teacher makes the poor student good and the good student superior. When our students fail, we, as teachers too, have failed.

—MARVA COLLINS

Everyone who remembers his own educational experience remembers teachers, not methods or techniques. The teacher is the kingpin of the educational situation. He makes or breaks the program.

—SIDNEY HOOK

One looks back with appreciation to the brilliant teachers, but with gratitude to those who touched our human feelings.

—CARL JUNG

She used to be a teacher but she has no class now.

—FRED ALLEN

You have become silly from teaching children! You have given them what little sense you have, and they give you all their stupidity.

—JOSEPH ROTH

Teachers are expected to reach unattainable goals with inadequate tools. The miracle is that at times they accomplish this impossible task.

—HAIM G. GINOTT

Teachers who educated children deserved more honor than parents who merely gave them birth; for bare life is furnished by the one, the other ensures a good life.

—ARISTOTLE

The teacher's life should have three periods—study until 25, investigation until 40, profession until 60, at which age I would have him retired on a double allowance.

—WILLIAM OSLER

We expect teachers to handle teenage pregnancy, substance abuse, and the failings of the family. Then we expect them to educate our children.

—JOHN SCULLEY

We teachers can only help the work going on, as servants wait upon a master.

—MARIA MONTESSORI

The task of universal, public, elementary education is still usually being conducted by a woman alone in a little room, presiding over a youthful distillate of a town or city. If she is willing, she tries to cultivate the minds of children both in good and desperate shape. Some of them have problems that she hasn't been trained to identify. She feels her way. She has no choice.

—TRACY KIDDER

Good teachers are costly, but bad teachers cost more.

—BOB TALBERT

Most teachers have little control over school policy or curriculum or choice of texts or special placement of students, but most have a great deal of autonomy inside their classroom. To a degree shared by only a few other occupations, such as police work, public education rests precariously on the skill and virtue of the people at the bottom of the institutional pyramid.

—TRACY KIDDER

Assistant masters came and went. Some liked little boys too little and some too much.

—EVELYN WAUGH

Every schoolmaster after the age of 49 is inclined to flatulence, is apt to swallow frequently, and to puff.

— HAROLD NICOLSON

Headmasters have powers at their disposal with which Prime ministers have never yet been invested.

— WINSTON CHURCHILL

I am inclined to think that one's education has been in vain if one fails to learn that most schoolmasters are idiots.

— HESKETH PERSON

It is when the gods hate a man with uncommon abhorrence that they drive him into the profession of schoolmaster.

— SENECA

No one ever got a word of sense out of any schoolmaster. You may, at a pinch, take their word about equilateral hexagons, but life, life's a closed book to them.

— JOHN MORTIMER

Whenever I look in the glass or see a photograph of myself, I am reminded of Petrarch's simple statement, "Nothing is more hideous than an old schoolmaster"!

— G. W. LYTTELTON

You sought the last resort of the feeble minds with classical educations. You became a schoolmaster.

—ALDOUS HUXLEY

Our civilization will break down if the schools fail to teach the incoming generation that there are some things that are not done.

—GAETANO SALVEMINI, Italian Fascist

Our job is not to make up anybody's mind, but to open minds and to make the agony of the decision-making so intense you can escape only by thinking.

—FRED FRIENDLY, recalling a quote seen on a blackboard years earlier when he was teaching

Teaching is an instinctual art, mindful of potential, craving of realizations, a pausing, seamless process.

—A. BARTLETT GIAMATTI

Who dares to teach must never cease to learn.

—JOHN COTTON DANA

I do not teach children, I give them joy.

—ISADORA DUNCAN

The secret of education is respecting the pupil.

—RALPH WALDO EMERSON

The art of teaching is the art of assisting discovery.

—MARK VAN DOREN

To teach is to learn twice.

—JOSEPH JOUBERT

Educate a man and you educate an individual—educate a woman and you educate a family.

—AGNES CRIPPS

Education has become too important to be left to educators.

—PETER DRUCKER

In the first place God made idiots. This was for practice. Then he made school boards.

—MARK TWAIN

Why in the world are salaries higher for administrators when the basic mission is teaching?

—JERRY BROWN

Some school officials have forgotten the reason they are there. Expediency and efficiency in administration have somehow become more important than educating children.

—MARIAN WRIGHT EDELMAN

I'm bilingual. I speak English and I speak educationese.

—SHIRLEY M. HUFSTEDLER

THINKING

I think I think; therefore, I think I am.

—AMBROSE BIERCE

Few people think more than two or three times a year; I have made an international reputation for myself by thinking once a week.

—GEORGE BERNARD SHAW

Thinking is the hardest work there is, which is the probable reason why so few engage in it.

—HENRY FORD

To think is to differ.

—CLARENCE DARROW

[Thinking is] what a great many people think they are doing when they are merely rearranging their prejudices.

—WILLIAM JAMES

If you think long you think wrong.

—JIM KAAT

If you can see further than today or tomorrow, if you can see further than that, then you're doing great.

—VAN MORRISON

Nothing pains some people more than having to think.

—MARTIN LUTHER KING, JR.

There's times when I just have to quit thinking . . . and the only way I can quit thinking is by shopping.

—TAMMY FAY BAKKER

You can lead a horse to water but you can't make him drink.

—ANONYMOUS

You can lead a whore to Vassar, but you can't make her think.

—DOROTHY PARKER

I teach only the truth—but that shouldn't make you believe it.

—MARTIN FISCHER

Men become civilized, not in proportion to their willingness to believe, but in proportion to their readiness to doubt.

—H. L. MENCKEN

I respect faith, but doubt is what gets you an education.

—WILSON MIZNER

Skepticism is the first step on the road to philosophy.

—DENIS DIDEROT

Just think of the tragedy of teaching children not to doubt.

—CLARENCE DARROW

The only means of strengthening one's intellect is to make up one's mind about nothing—to let the mind be a thoroughfare for all thoughts.

—JOHN KEATS

100

If you leave the smallest corner of your head vacant for a moment, other people's opinions will rush in from all quarters.

—GEORGE BERNARD SHAW

It is not enough to have a good mind; the main thing is to use it well.

—RENÉ DESCARTES

Minds are like parachutes: they only function when open.

—THOMAS R. DEWAR

Poverty of good is easily cured: poverty of the mind is irreparable.

—MICHEL EYQUEM DE MONTAIGNE

A mind is a terrible thing to waste.

—United Negro College Fund slogan

What a waste it is to lose one's mind—or not to have a mind. How true that is.

—DAN QUAYLE, speaking to the United Negro College Fund

Quayle taught the kids a valuable lesson: if you don't study you could end up Vice President.

—JAY LENO

All men should strive
to learn before they die
what they are running from, and to, and why.

—JAMES THURBER

Uses of
Education

Theodore Roosevelt said thorough knowledge of the Bible was worth more than a college education. A thorough knowledge of anything is worth more than a college education.

—YALE *Record*

The primary purpose of a liberal education is to make one's mind a pleasant place to spend one's time.

—SYDNEY J. HARRIS

The test and the use of man's education is that he finds pleasure in the exercise of his mind.

—JACQUES BARZUN

The educational process has no end beyond itself; it is its own end.

—JOHN DEWEY

The use of a university is to make young gentlemen as unlike their fathers as possible.

—WOODROW WILSON

College is always on the road to somewhere else.

—TOM ROBBINS

Is it necessary to have read Spinoza in order to make out a laundry list?

—JEANNE DETOURBEY

Education helps earning capacity. Ask any college professor.

—HERBERT V. PROCHNOW

A liberal-arts education is supposed to provide you with a value system, a standard, a set of ideas, not a job.

—CAROLINE BIRD

The more that learn to read the less learn how to make a living. That's one thing about a little education. It spoils you for actual work. The more you know the more you think somebody owes you a living.

—WILL ROGERS

The advantage of a classical education is that it enables you to despise the wealth which it prevents you from achieving.

—RUSSELL GREEN

The only difference between intelligence and education is this: intelligence will make you a good living.

—CHARLES F. KETTERING

I learned law so well, the day I graduated I sued the college, won the case, and got my tuition back.

—FRED ALLEN

A man who has never gone to school may steal from a freight car; but if he has a university education, he may steal the whole railroad.

—THEODORE ROOSEVELT

Society produces rogues, and education makes one rogue cleverer than another.

—OSCAR WILDE

College novices, who think they know everything in their cloisters, and that all the learning lies in books, make dismal figures when they come into the world.

—SAMUEL RICHARDSON

No matter who you are or what you plan to do, learn to type!

—LIZ SMITH

Education makes people easy to lead, but difficult to drive; easy to govern, but impossible to enslave.

—HENRY PETER, Lord Brougham

I didn't go to high school and I didn't go to grade school, either. Education, I think, is for refinement and is probably a liability.

—H. L. HUNT

In the old days men studied for the sake of self-improvement; nowadays men study in order to impress other people.

—CONFUCIUS

A college education shows a man how little other people know.

—THOMAS CHANDLER HALIBURTON

The aim of a college education is to teach you to know a good man when you see one.

—WILLIAM JAMES

Education doesn't change life much. It just lifts trouble to a higher plane of regard.

—ROBERT FROST

I think it would be a wonderful thing if a coach could just forget all about the high school and prep school wonders of the world and develop a team from among the students of his institution who came to his school because they liked it best and not because of any attractive offers made for athletic ability.

—KNUTE ROCKNE

VARSITY
SPORTS

Every priest and nun in the country is a potential recruiter. When I was an eighth grader at St. Mary's in Poughkeepsie, New York, the nun used to line us up to say a prayer for Notre Dame.

—MONTY STICKLES, former Notre Dame tight end

If no one else had, Notre Dame would surely have invented football later on.

—DAN JENKINS

I certainly wasn't smart enough to get in academically . . . I guess the standards for being a coach are lower.

—LOU HOLTZ, Notre Dame football coach

There are two kinds of people in the world, Notre Dame lovers and Notre Dame haters. And, quite frankly, they're both a pain in the ass.

—DAN DEVINE, former Notre Dame football coach

If coaches are to have stability and security, they need to be treated like an English professor.

—JOE PATERNO

We're trying to build a university our football team can be proud of.

—DR GEORGE L. CROSS, president, University of Oklahoma

If you asked the alumni if they'd rather have a Nobel prize–winning graduate or a Heisman Trophy winner, 95 percent would take the Heisman.

—BEANO COOK

My motto is to keep 'em hungry. I like 'em sullen, but not mutinous.

—HERMAN HICKMAN, Yale football coach on alumni

Cattle have no alumni.

—PHIL CUTCHIN, Oklahoma State football coach, on why he quit to become a cattle rancher

Monday through Friday they want you to be like Harvard. On Saturday they want you to play like Oklahoma.

—JIM VALVANO, on college administrators

The last thing in the world a college or university should be concerned with is being number one in football or basketball if the price one pays for that is the corruption of character and the undermining of true student morale on campus.

—HOWARD COSELL

I certainly don't think football is as important as English or some other academic department, except that it's pretty hard to get a crowd out to watch an examination. It's pretty hard to rally 'round a math class.

—BEAR BRYANT

A school without football is in danger of deteriorating into a medieval study hall.

—VINCE LOMBARDI

College football is becoming so complicated, players find it a recreation to go to classes.

—T. S. ELIOT

Academe, *n.* An ancient school where morality and philosophy were taught.

Academy, *n.* (from academe). A modern school where football is taught.

—AMBROSE BIERCE

It was like a heart transplant. We tried to implant college in him, but his head rejected it.

—BARRY SWITZER, on a player who dropped out of school

I believe in higher education. You know, 6'8", 6'9", 6'10".

—SMOKEY GAINES, San Diego State basketball coach

Although I never played football, I made many contributions. I went to the University of Southern

California in the late 1940s and took the English exams for all the Trojan linemen.

—ART BUCHWALD

Most of us are out of public high schools like everyone else. We're the same kind of football players who go to UCLA, except we can read.

—MIKE WYMAN, Stanford defensive lineman

The position of UCLA and USC in athletics is like the Arabs in oil. By a quirk of nature, they're sitting on 50 percent of the world's supply.

—GEORGE REVELING, Washington State basketball coach

We'd like our receivers to have both, but if they had both, they'd be at USC.

—LAVELL EDWARDS, Brigham Young football coach, when asked whether BYU receivers had speed or quickness

But the real tragedy was that fifteen hadn't been colored in yet.

—STEVE SPURRIER, Florida State football coach, commenting on a fire at Auburn's football dorm that destroyed twenty books.

I'm honored that you invited me, especially when for $10,000 and a new convertible you could have had the top running-back prospect at SMU.

—TOM BROKAW, speaking at an NCAA honors luncheon

Does college pay? Of course. If you're a halfback or a basketball player they pay you very well. College athletes are always saying to me, "When should I turn pro?" And I say not until you've earned all you can in college.

—WILL ROGERS

The education is never completed until he dies.

—ROBERT E. LEE

EPITAPHS

My education began with a set of blocks which had on them the Roman numerals and the letters of the alphabet. It is not yet finished.

—CALVIN COOLIDGE

I am learning all the time. The tombstone will be my diploma.

—EARTHA KITT

Die, and endow a college, or a cat.

—ALEXANDER POPE

INDEX

Abdelnaby, Alaa, 57
Adams, Henry Brooks, 29, 54, 93
Addison, Joseph, 27
Ade, George, 46
Alcott, A. B., 66
Allen, Fred, 94, 103
Allen, Woody, 23, 52, 76
Alther, Lisa, 36
Altman, Jeff, 58
Amsterdam, Anthony, 64
Andrea, Christopher, 42
anonymous, 6, 11, 92, 99
Anthony, Susan B., 88
Aristotle, 25, 94
Arnold, Kevin, 24
Ashton-Warner, Sylvia, 8
Asquith, Margot, 44
Astor, Nancy, 67
Atkinson, Brooks, 18
Auden, W. H., 70
Azikiwe, Nnamdi, 35

Bagley, Desmond, 17
Baker, Russell, 12, 78
Bakker, Tammy Fay, 99
Baldwin, James, 73
Balfour, Arthur, 22
Bankhead, Tallulah, 27
Barber, Benjamin R., 74, 77
Barnes, Marvin, 17
Barrie, J. M., 81
Barry, Dave, 22, 23
Barzun, Jacques, 90, 92, 102
Beals, Jennifer, 83
Bean, Orson, 38

Beecher, Henry Ward, 42
Beerbohm, Max, 88
Belushi, John, 22
Benchley, Robert, 56
Bennett, William J., 15, 18, 70
Benson, A. C., 44
Berman, Shelley, 23
Bernard, Claude, 55
Bierce, Ambrose, 26, 44, 56, 98, 107
Billings, Josh, 51, 56
Bird, Caroline, 103
Birnbach, Lisa, 37, 89
Blount, Roy, Jr., 49, 58
Bly, Carol, 11
Boas, George, 25
Bok, Derek, 43
Bombeck, Erma, 15
Boren, James H., 70
Boyden, Frank L., 89
Boyle, Hal, 70
Brandeis, Louis, 29
Brock, William, 40
Brodie, Peter, 21
Brokaw, Tom, 108
Bronowski, Jacob, 91
Brontë, Charlotte, 67
Brown, Gates, 82
Brown, Jerry, 74, 98
Bryan, William Jennings, 70
Bryant, Bear, 107
Buchwald, Art, 108
Buckley, William F., Jr., 49
Bukowski, Charles, 51
Bulwer-Lytton, Edward, 4, 55
Burke, Edmund, 73

111

Burns, George, 41
Bush, George, 5, 78
Butler, Nicholas Murray, 1
Butler, Samuel, 55, 71

Cable, George Washington, 56
Callahan, Sidney, 6
Campbell, Elden, 38
Capote, Truman, 35
Capp, Al, 31
Carroll, Lewis, 58, 75
Cascone, Gina, 84
Cavett, Dick, 61, 85
Chaplin, Charlie, 25
Chatham (Ont.) *News*, 8
Chesson, John, 45
Chesterfield, Lord, 57
Chesterton, G. K., 5, 21, 25, 29, 62, 63,
    66, 87, 89
Chinese proverb, 64
Churchill, Winston, 20, 54, 96
Ciardi, John, 17, 33
Cicero, Marcus Tullius, 22
Clark, Kenneth B., 7
Clarke, Arthur C., 36
Clarke, Hendrik John, 62
Clemenceau, Georges, 55
Coffman, Lotus Delat, 16
Cohen, Julius, 58
Colby, Frank Moore, 62
Collins, Marva, 82, 93
Colton, Charles Caleb, 35
Conant, James Bryant, 3
Confucius, 104
Cook, Beano, 106
Coolidge, Calvin, 109
Cooper, Roger, 88
Cortines, Ramon, 56
Cosell, Howard, 106
Cousins, Norman, 69
Coward, Noel, 46
Cripps, Agnes, 98
Crisp, Quentin, 81
Cross, Dr. George L., 106
Cutchin, Phil, 106

da Vinci, Leonardo, 60
Dana, John Cotton, 97

Dana, Richard Henry, 31
Darrow, Clarence, 99, 100
Davies, Robertson, 47, 78
Davis, Mac, 82
Davis, Ossie, 46, 70
De Mille, Agnes, 86
De Vries, Peter, 14, 32
Dean, Dizzy, 8
Descartes, René, 101
Detourbey, Jeanne, 102
Devine, Dan, 105
Dewar, Thomas R., 101
Dewey, John, 2, 54, 102
Diderot, Denis, 100
Dionysius, 23
Disraeli, Benjamin, 16
Dobie, Frank J., 45
Dole, Robert, 40
Douglass, Frederick, 53
Douvan, Elizabeth, 19
Doyle, Arthur Conan, 50
Drucker, Peter, 15, 65, 98
DuBois, W. E. B., 16
Dulles, John Foster, 90
Dumas, Alexandre, 6
Duncan, Isadora, 97
Dunne, Peter Finley, 60
Durant, Will, 29
Dylan, Bob, 18, 85

Eban, Abba, 22
Edelman, Marian Wright, 5, 98
Edison, Thomas Alva, 34
Edman, Irwin, 26
Edwards, Lavell, 108
Einstein, Albert, 23, 37, 50, 66, 80
Eisenhower, Dwight D., 45, 84
Eliot, George, 10
Eliot, T. S., 107
Ellis, Havelock, 81
Ellison, Harlan, 43
Emerson, Ralph Waldo, 30, 86, 90, 97
Euripides, 37

Feather, William, 25
Feiffer, Jules, 13
Fielding, Henry, 87, 88
Fillmore, Millard, 40

Fischer, Martin, 100
Fitzgerald, F. Scott, 36, 50
Ford, Henry, 51, 99
Forster, E. M., 63
Franklin, Benjamin, 21, 92
Freeman, Morgan, 24
Freud, Anna, 35
Freud, Sigmund, 36
Friendly, Fred, 97
Fromm, Erich, 7
Frost, Robert, 12, 25, 72, 90, 105
Fulghum, Robert, 8
Fuller, R. Buckminster, 34
Fussell, Paul, 1

Gaines, Smokey, 107
Galbraith, John Kenneth, 41
Galsworthy, John, 78
Gardner, John W., 63
Geisel, Theodore (Dr. Seuss), 31
Giamatti, A. Bartlett, 15, 97
Gide, André, 52
Gilman, Charlotte Perkins, 69
Ginott, Haim G., 94
Gobel, George, 20
Godwin, Gail, 61
Goethe, Johann Wolfgang von, 46, 51
Goheen, Robert F., 17
Goldberg, Isaac, 8
Goldman, Emma, 7
Golic, Bob, 38
Gorky, Maxim, 80
Gould, Samuel B., 91
Graziano, Rocky, 8
Green, Celia, 60
Green, Russell, 103
Greene, Graham, 22
Griffith, Calvin, 38

Haas, Charles, 63
Half, Robert, 32
Haliburton, Thomas Chandler, 104
Halifax, Lord, 92
Halliburton, Richard, 37
Hamilton, Edith, 30
Harris, Sydney J., 1, 40, 102
Harrison, Jerry, 49
Haskins, Henry S., 55

Haughton, Rosemary, 24
Hayakawa, S. I., 91
Hazlitt, William, 53
Hegel, G. W. Friedrich, 64
Heine, Heinrich, 21, 32
Hendren, L. L., 18
Henry, Will, 60
Heraclitus, 51
Herold, Don, 55
Hesburgh, Theodore, 46, 91
Hickman, Herman, 106
Hildebrand, Joel, 35
Hirsch, E. D., Jr., 66
Hitler, Adolf, 50, 74
Hoffman, Abbie, 20
Hoffman, Dustin, 38
Hofstadter, Richard, 1
Holder, Geoffrey, 4
Holtz, Lou, 105
Holmes, Oliver Wendell, Jr., 30
Holmes, Oliver Wendell, Sr., 33, 45
Hook, Sidney, 93
Horace, 52
Horton, Miles, 26
Howe, Edgar W., 5, 81
Howe, Harold, 19
Hubbard, Elbert, 3, 20, 65, 71, 72, 87
Hudson, Virginia Cary, 76
Hufstedler, Shirley M., 98
Humphrey, Hubert, 69
Hunt, H. L., 104
Hutchins, Robert Maynard, 16, 43, 49
Huxley, Aldous, 6, 22, 97
Huxley, T. H., 53, 71

Ingersoll, Robert G., 17
Irving, Washington, 51

Jackson, Holbrook, 55
James, Alice, 27
James, William, 33, 52, 99, 104
Japanese proverb, 5
Jefferson, Thomas, 75
Jenkins, Dan, 105
Johannot, Louis, 6
Johnson, Betsey, 85
Johnson, Lyndon B., 2, 42, 73
Johnson, Samuel, 10, 13

Jones, T. A. D., 47
Jordan, Barbara, 73
Jordan, Michael, 84
Joubert, Joseph, 97
Jugo, Miguel de Unamuno y, 24
Jung, Carl, 94

Kaat, Jim, 99
Karras, Alex, 37
Kazin, Alfred, 21
Kearney, Bobm, 43
Keats, John, 100
Keeney, Barnaby, 14, 18
Keller, Helen, 67
Kennedy, John F., 3, 41, 49, 74
Kerr, Clark, 19
Kerr, Jean, 8
Kettering, Charles F., 103
Keynes, John Maynard, 26
Kibbee, Robert J., 14
Kidder, Tracy, 72, 95
Kierkegaard, Søren, 63
King, Martin Luther, Jr., 99
King, Stephen, 11
Kissinger, Henry, 72
Kitt, Eartha, 109
Kozol, Jonathan, 85

Lane, Margaret, 60
Lao-Tse, 53
Law, Vernon, 33
Le Shan, Eda J., 74
Leacock, Stephen, 20, 44
Lee, Robert E., 109
Leibowitz, Fran, 6, 12, 77, 80
Lennon, John, 34, 83
Leno, Jay, 101
Lessing, Doris, 54
Levenson, Sam, 35
Levinson, Leonard L., 17
Lewin, Roger, 64
Lewis, Sinclair, 77
Lichtenberg, Georg Christoph, 33
Limbaugh, Rush, 27, 63
Lincoln, Abraham, 14
Lippmann, Walter, 3
Little, Mary Wilson, 60
Locke, John, 75

Lodge, David, 37
Lombardi, Vince, 107
Lorti, Dan, 2
Loud, Pat, 19
Lowell, Abbott Lawrence, 16
Lubbock, John, 54
Luther, Martin, 70
Lyttelton, G. W., 96

Macchiarola, Frank, 74
MacLeish, Archibald, 44, 64
Malcolm X, 76
Malraux, André, 13
Mano, D. Keith, 47
Mann, Horace, 26
Marshall, Thurgood, 30
Marx, Groucho, 76
Masters, Dr. William H., 24
Matisse, Henri, 34
Matthews, Brander, 21, 46
Maugham, Somerset, 56
McAuliffe, Christa, 93
McGuire, Al, 32, 57
Mead, Margaret, 65, 71
Melville, Herman, 32
Mencken, H. L., 1, 36, 51, 71, 88, 100
Miller, Henry, 20
Mills, Carol, 3
Mizner, Wilson, 60, 100
Montague, Ashley, 62
Montaigne, Michel Eyquem de, 30, 69, 101
Montessori, Maria, 67, 95
Moodie, Susanna, 69
Morley, Robert, 88
Morrison, Van, 99
Mortimer, John, 96

Nabokov, Vladimir, 71
Naipaul, V. S., 3
Nance, Jim, 47
Nash, Ogden, 12, 80
Neuwirth, Bebe, 78
Nicholson, Jack, 84
Nicolson, Harold, 96
Nixon, Richard, 2, 84

O'Connor, Flannery, 77
Olgilvy, David, 14

Oppenheimer, J. Robert, 17
Osborne, John, 92
Osler, William, 94

Paderewski, Ignace Jan, 34
Paine, Thomas, 42
Parker, Dorothy, 86, 100
Paterno, Joe, 106
Peltason, Jack, 41
Pennington, James W. C., 73
Percy, Walker, 58
Perkins, James, 16
Person, Hesketh, 96
Peter, Henry, Lord Brougham, 104
Peter, Lawrence J., 67
Phelps, William Lyon, 65
Plato, 64
Pompidou, Georges, 90
Pope, Alexander, 4, 53, 109
Popper, Karl, 42
Pound, Ezra, 13, 29
Prince Charles, 78
Princess Anne, 4
Prochnow, Herbert V., 102

Quayle, Dan, 57, 101
Quindlen, Anna, 82
Quisenberry, Dan, 58

Reagan, Ronald, 67, 74
Renan, Ernest, 24
Reston, Sally and James, 5
Reveling, George, 108
Richardson, Samuel, 104
Robbins, Tom, 102
Roby, Peter, 47
Rockne, Knute, 105
Rogers, Rutherford D., 56
Rogers, Will, 42, 43, 77, 87, 103,
     109
Roosevelt, Eleanor, 73
Roosevelt, Franklin, 29
Roosevelt, Theodore, 42, 103
Roth, Joseph, 94
Rudnick, Paul, 46, 61
Ruskin, John, 66
Russell, Bertrand, 43, 80
Russell, David L., 32

Sahl, Mort, 47
Saki (H. H. Munro), 86
Salinger, J. D., 92
Salvemini, Gaetano, 97
Santayana, George, 4, 31
Saroyan, William, 52
Sarton, May, 16
Savage, Fred, 11
Savile, George, 53
Sawyer, Diane, 82
saying, 63
Schreiner, Olive, 87
Schulz, Charles, 4
Schweitzer, Albert, 45
Sculley, John, 94
Seeger, Pete, 31
Sendak, Maurice, 81
Seneca, 96
Shakespeare, William, 10
Sharpe, Tom, 53
Shaw, George Bernard, 7, 10, 21, 23, 30,
     45, 92, 98, 101
Silber, John, 41
Simmel, George, 26
Simmons, Gene, 85
Simon, Neil, 61
Simpson, Alan, 44
Sinatra, Frank, 49
Skinner, B. F., 26, 37
Smith, Lillian, 51, 52
Smith, Liz, 104
Southey, Robert, 75
Spark, Muriel, 62, 65
Spurrier, Steve, 108
Stein, Gertrude, 34
Stein, Leo, 62
Stickles, Monty, 105
Stone, I. F., 87
Streep, Meryl, 83
Sullivan, Annie, 7
Swift, Jonathan, 33
Switzer, Barry, 107
Szaz, Thomas, 93

Taft, William Howard, 40
Talbert, Bob, 66, 95
Talleyrand, Charles Maurice de, 54
Tey, Josephine, 46

Thoreau, Henry David, 35
Thurber, James, 51, 101
Toom, Andrei, 40, 66
Trevelyan, G. M., 26
Trillin, Calvin, 46, 57, 58, 61, 80
Truman, Harry, 30
Twain, Mark, 10, 13, 20, 31, 55, 65, 75, 98

Updike, John, 47, 86
Ustinov, Peter, 89

Valéry, Paul, 24
Valvano, Jim, 106
Van Doren, Mark, 97
Vanderbilt, Cornelius, 27
Vaughan, Bill, 18
Veeck, Bill, 32
Vidal, Gore, 77, 78
Von Hoffman, Nicholas, 10
Vonnegut, Kurt, 11

Walker, Johnny, 57
Wallace, George, 49
Walters, Vernon A., 1
Ward, William Arthur, 61
Waugh, Evelyn, 89, 95
Weil, Simone, 72

Welles, Orson, 15
Wells, H. G., 27, 53
Welty, Eudora, 7
West, Nathaniel, 80
White, E. B., 34
White, Patrick, 54
White, Vanna, 43
White, William Allen
Wiggam, Albert Edward, 36
Wilde, Oscar, 25, 27, 32, 52, 60, 64, 91, 103
Will, George, 15
Wilson, Woodrow, 90, 102
Winfrey, Oprah, 76
Wise, Stephen S., 2
Wittgenstein, Ludvig, 23
Wood, David, 19
Wooden, John, 55
Wright, Frank Lloyd, 50
Wylie, Philip, 93
Wyman, Mike, 108

Yale *Record*, 102
Yates, Richard, 44
Yeats, William Butler, 62
Yutang, Lin, 67

Zenobius, 91